BLAIR'S BR

BLAIR'S BRITAIN

A CHRISTIAN CRITIQUE

MARK D. CHAPMAN

DARTON · LONGMAN + TODD

For my parents

First published in 2005 by
Darton, Longman and Todd Ltd
1 Spencer Court
140–142 Wandsworth High Street
London SW18 4JJ

ISBN 0–232–52603–6

A catalogue record for this book is available
from the British Library

Phototypeset by Intype Libra Ltd
Printed and bound in Great Britain by
The Cromwell Press, Trowbridge, Wiltshire

CONTENTS

Preface   vii

1 The Old and the New   1
2 Community   12
3 Management   30
4 Theologies of Community and Theologies of Conflict   43
5 Communities and Pluralism   59
6 Communities, Civil Society and the Reconstruction
   of Politics   71
7 Another Christian Politics: Pluralist Democracy   83

Notes   101
Bibliography   112
Index   119

PREFACE

This book has been a long time gestating. The idea stems from a lecture I was asked to give in memory of J. N. Figgis at Marnhull in Dorset in 1999 on the eightieth anniversary of his death. This was the first time I had thought about pluralism and New Labour, although I had been thinking about Figgis ever since I heard Rowan Williams speak on him when I was a graduate student at Oxford. Bits of that original talk have found their way into this book. Various other invitations in England and South Africa got me thinking about political theory and its relationships with theology. I am grateful to all those who thought my ideas worth hearing and who offered feedback, especially the members of the Scripture, Theology and Society Group, and also Michael Brierley and Mongezi Guma. Some of the material has been published in different forms elsewhere. I am grateful for permission to use the following: 'Tony Blair, J. N. Figgis and the State of the Future' in *Studies in Christian Ethics* 13:2 (2000), pp. 49–66; 'Pluralism, Welfare and the "Common Good": Three Varieties of Christian Socialism' in *Political Theology* 2 (2000), pp. 33–56; 'The Social Doctrine of the Trinity: Some Problems' in *Anglican Theological Review* 83:2 (2001), pp. 239–54; 'Management and Community: Some Problems with New Labour' in *Political Theology* 4 (2003), pp. 192–205; 'Ronald Preston, William Temple, and the Future of Christian Politics' in *Studies in Christian Ethics* 17:2 (2004), pp. 162–72; *Building Community in South Africa: A Christian Perspective*, Johannesburg: Ecumenical Services for Socio-Economic Transformation, 2003; and 'Pluralism and Moral Regeneration: Building Community in South African Perspective' in *Journal of Theology for Southern Africa* 119 (July 2004), pp. 4–14.

A few other thanks are due. As always my wife, Linda, has listened to me, seemingly attentively and usually disagreeing, and my boys,

Jacob and Edmund, are showing a healthy interest in answering back about politics and religion. But a special debt of thanks is due to my father, Len, who was once the youngest Labour councillor in England and who first awakened my interest in socialist politics. He now proudly possesses a framed letter from Tony Blair written in gratitude for fifty years' loyal service to the party. He is also a devout catholic Christian. We often disagree, but, as this book shows, disagreement is at the heart of a functioning democracy. It is to him and to my mother, Kathleen, who has supported us both, that this book is affectionately dedicated.

CHAPTER 1

The Old and the New

Introduction: 1 May 1997

The events of 1 May 1997 are etched on my memory. It was the day of the General Election when the Labour Party at long last stood a realistic chance of winning. But as the polling stations were opening at 7 a.m. I had my mind on something else. I was on my way to church to celebrate the Eucharist in honour of the apostles, St Philip and St James – in the Church of England the feast has remained on May Day, the traditional beginning of summer, and also, and quite coincidentally, International Labour Day. Whereas the Roman Catholic Church had sought to usurp the great workers' festival with its invention in 1955 of the feast of St Joseph the Worker (which meant that it had to move the two apostles first to 11 May and then to 3 May in 1969), the calendar of the Church of England kept Pip and Jim on 1 May. Ecclesiastical custom meant that I was able to wear red vestments on 1 May – and this seemed doubly appropriate for a long-time socialist on that particular day, when it looked likely that the Labour Party would win the General Election after 18 years of more or less incompetent rule by the Conservatives. There was a tangible sense of expectation and excitement throughout the day – and like many others I stayed up through the night to watch one Tory after another fall from power. The Southgate moment, when Michael Portillo lost his safe seat to the young gay Stephen Twigg, was truly memorable (if almost unbelievable). Portillo did at least display honour in defeat as he presumably began to realise that he might have a more lucrative career in the media and that the Conservative Party did not offer such good prospects.

As I prayed in church before the service on this very particular May Day I found it impossible not to reflect on the strange ambiguities of the sacred and secular, on that combination of the

world-forsaking first disciples and the worldliness of socialist politics. Immediately, the historic resonances of 1 May took me back to
my childhood. I could vividly remember television images of the
great demonstrations of military might in the pre-1989 days of
Soviet power, the long processions of tanks and soldiers before the
grand old men of the Soviet regime who stood motionless on their
Moscow balcony. As an impressionable schoolboy I would regu-
larly read the gratis copy of *Soviet Weekly* sent to my grammar
school library. It colourfully recorded the achievements of the
Motherland, celebrating tractor technology, inter-ethnic harmony
and successful five-year plans. I was somewhat naïvely caught up in
the socialist myths, rooted as they were in martyrdom, universal
brotherhood and other laudable ideals.

At the same time I was also an enthusiastic (and equally impressionable) altar boy in my local Anglo-Catholic church. Here I was
inducted into the great tradition of Christian Socialism and the
Jubilee group, then in its radical infancy. As I lapped it all up
(together with a very conservative theology) I became increasingly
aware of the similarities between socialism and Christianity, a feeling that was reinforced when the head server gave me a copy of
Mervyn Stockwood's naïve and in many ways ridiculous little
book, *The Cross and the Sickle*.[1] However much the messages of
both socialism and Christianity might have been corrupted through
the centuries of hypocrisy and double-talk (and Stockwood himself was not without more than a little of both), something of the
ideals of the founders of both Christianity and socialism still
seemed important. In the past there had so often been a willingness
on both sides to stand up and be counted. Indeed, it seemed to me
that socialists often used the Christian vocabulary of discipleship
and expected the same kind of commitment, and they spoke of
being prepared to die for the sake of the new Jerusalem – the red
flag shrouded oft its martyrs dead. Socialists – and for that matter
Conservatives – spoke the language of high ideals and expected
commitment.

As I celebrated the Eucharist on 1 May 1997 I remember
trembling with excitement, but at the same time I had a more
rational sense of fear. This was the fear of a frustration that stemmed
from my perception of a profound tragedy at the heart of modern
politics: the martyrs' vision, the cost of radical discipleship, did not
seem to figure in mainstream politics at all. The great values of

fraternity, solidarity and co-operation which had underpinned the socialist vision right through its history had been transformed into something quite different. And I wasn't quite sure that the Labour Party's socialism was the kind of socialism I really wanted (I had already resigned my membership of the party over Labour's uncritical support of the bombing of Iraq during the first Gulf War).

That resignation was not just a knee-jerk reaction to what seemed an excessive use of force. It was also a very personal response to my experience of Labour Party politics. I had spent much of the mid-1980s attending evening meetings of the local Labour Party and gradually I convinced myself that I was simply not a party man. I could not bear ambitious people nor being told what to think. But at a deeper level I also began to question many of the sacred cows of socialism – even the National Health Service as it had developed out of the post-war ideal of universal healthcare. So much of what seemed to be important, and so many of the great ideals which had moulded the original visionaries behind socialist politics, had disappeared. On the one hand, there was the frightening Kafkaesque bureaucracy responsible for planning and target-setting, and, on the other hand, there seemed to be the loss of any meaningful sense of local participation, of what might be called face-to-face fraternity.

The ideals of New Labour seemed to go even further in diluting the socialist vision. Indeed, New Labour spent much of its time lampooning the old socialist values as outmoded and old and replacing them with new, ever vaguer ideals of something called 'community'. This went hand in hand with other hazy ideals like decency and efficient, high quality economic management. Passion seemed to have been excised in the name of efficiency. That seemed to me to be a great tragedy, and even to starve politics of its sense of hope and its longing for change. For the Christian Socialist this would be the final death-blow: after all, a vision lies at the heart of Christian faith and provides the basis for hope and for transformation. Without hope of transformation, politics becomes little more than another name for competent economic management and efficiency which seem quite detached from the great Christian vision of unconditional love of neighbour.

In my view, political commitment is an expression of the same sort of vision, corrupted no doubt by power and social and economic constraints and often simply masking a will-to-power, but nevertheless still something able to express a possibility that the world can be changed. The parody of socialism in the May Day parades did not mean that the socialist vision was dead, any more than the parody of Christianity in the power-mongering of the Borgia popes or a hundred and one other atrocities meant that the Christian vision was robbed of all content. After all, it was for the vision of a better world that the apostles were prepared to die. It is for the sake of the vision that I have written this book – it is often quite personal and relates to my own real struggle to relate the political to the theological, but it also tries to engage in detail and more dispassionately with some of the underlying values of modern British politics, especially in the current Labour Party.

What I offer in this book is an attempt to understand what has happened since that extraordinary May Day in 1997 when the political complexion of Britain was decisively transformed. As I seek to explain what has taken place so I will challenge many of the presuppositions of the political system: questions will be raised about the role of the state, the nature of sovereignty and the meaning of community. I seek to expose the values at the heart of the New Labour project for what they are, and at the same time I try to explain the widespread loss of political participation and offer remedies for the future. There is much that is critical, but it is criticism rooted in the attempt to conceive a form of Christian socialism which moves in a very different direction from that taken by New Labour.

The book begins with a brief account of the pre-Blairite Labour Party, and of the welfare consensus of the old collectivist state that dominated so much of the 1950s through to the 1970s. After raising questions about the feasibility of this model in the contemporary world, and challenging the theological assumptions of some of its Christian defenders, I move on in Chapter 2 to discuss the alternative model offered by New Labour: I start with a lengthy account of the nature of 'community', since this has proved to be one of the most important values of New Labour, but it is also at the same time one of the most elusive. After outlining some of the problems inherent in Christian defences of community, I move on in Chapter 3 to tackle the second major value of New Labour: the independence of the economic, the politics of audit, and the cult of management. This chapter carefully surveys the persuasiveness of political rhetoric and the management of public discourse. Here words like efficiency and management become ciphers for a kind of centralisation and control which serves to stifle creativity and human flourishing. This subtle manipulation of discourse leads to a serious reduction of the sphere of the political, and inexorably towards a decline in participation in the political process. Quite simply there is less and less for politicians to do. Chapter 4 moves to a discussion of the relationships between theological and political language, especially the so-called social doctrine of the Trinity. Chapters 5 and 6 analyse the importance of pluralism, especially the relationships between the national community and the outsider in a post-September 11 world. Here I return to some of the issues raised in Chapter 2 in relation to the nature of community, pluralism and the common good. These are shown to be particularly pressing in connection to the creation of enemies and outsiders.

While this could be a depressing book, it does not seek to be so – the final chapter explores alternative ways forward for a Christian politics. Drawing on some relatively unknown thinkers from the English political pluralist tradition of the early years of the twentieth century I offer a vision of a participatory politics which bears more than a passing resemblance to some moderate forms of anarchism. All this I see as rooted in an eclectic yet fundamentally orthodox and realistic Christian theology. It will become clear that in my view there can still be a Christian politics, and what I offer is a political vision that is at heart both socialist and democratic. At the same time, however, it is one that is far removed from the general thrust of New Labour politics. My hope, such as it is, is that this might help reinvigorate political debate among Christians, and perhaps even among those socialists left in the Labour Party.

The Old and the New

In the years immediately before 1997 much of the political language in the Labour Party was dominated by talk of 'the New'.[2] This received an even greater boost after the election victory. It was a word repeated so often that it began to stick: the old collectivist visions which, to many members of the Party, had reached their sell-by date had made way for a new version of Labour politics quite different from what had gone before. Among the younger generation of leaders there was a constant effort to redefine the fundamental characteristics of socialism – and often a reluctance to use the word 'socialism' altogether – in the search for a new sense of identity for the Labour Party: for some, even the spatial metaphors of left and right no longer seemed relevant.

'Modernisation' quickly became the key term for New Labour, even though what actually constituted 'the modern' often lacked coherence and became little more than vague rhetoric. If it had any meaning it seemed to imply a position somewhere in the political centre, a kind of balancing act between the extremes of what had gone before. Being modern had to do with reclaiming the central ground which had been sacrificed at the altar of ideological purity. As Tony Blair put it soon after his election as leader of the Labour Party following John Smith's death in 1994: 'The solutions of neither the old Left nor the new Right will do. We need a radical centre in modern politics . . . And today's Labour party – New Labour – is a party of the centre as well as the centre-left.'[3] Similarly, in his speech to the 1994 Labour Party Conference at Blackpool, Tony Blair boldly proclaimed: 'Our party – New Labour. Our mission – New Britain. New Labour: New Britain.'[4] Not surprisingly, the central slogan for the 1997 General Election campaign was for 'New Labour, New Britain', a phrase that pointed to the virtues of modernisation and youth and which was plastered across the country and in the rear windscreens of many thousands of cars.

The crusty Old Labour image of trade union officials in ill-fitting grey suits bargaining in smoke-filled rooms, and the disastrous industrial relations of the 1970s, which seemed to stifle economic development, made way for the dynamism of youth. There had to be new and better ways of doing things. This youthful image was epitomised by the leader himself. Tony Blair was a young, good-looking, privately educated middle-class barrister, who seemed quite different from any of his predecessors, and who, it seems, had never had much to do with trade unionism at all. His only claim to street credibility was having played electric guitar as a student. For Blair and his modernising colleagues newness was about throwing off the legacy of the past and zealously replacing it with a vision of a new political order. Times had changed, and politics had to change alongside. In particular this meant reform of the old collectivist ethos of Labour politics symbolically enshrined in the 'common ownership' of the old Clause Four of the Party Constitution. This was the touchstone of the old party and continued to be printed on Labour Party membership cards until the 1990s. After a painful but ultimately successful political battle it was modified by Tony Blair into something far less concrete. For the New Labour Party, modernisation involved moving away from collectivism and common ownership towards the far vaguer talk of 'community' and 'tolerance', words which were finally incorporated in the statement agreed by the Labour Party National Executive Committee on 13 March 1995.[5]

One of the most useful aspects of Blairite political rhetoric is its imprecision: the 'new' of New Labour lacked much definitive content, at least at the beginning. Few ventured to say precisely what a new community might look like. Far more important than any positive content was the contrast with the old: a host of different forms of labourism could be included in the umbrella term of old, all of which could then be regarded as in some sense passé, or at the very least in need of serious reform. Although Neil Kinnock had won his bitter battles with the Militant Tendency in the 1980s which had led to the expulsion of the Old Trotskyism, he had not sought fundamentally to challenge the moderate socialism of the 1960s and 70s. The Blairite rhetoric of the 'new', however, was able to tar everything old with the same brush – and that even included the old welfare consensus.

This welfare model was the dominant form of mainstream Labour thinking in the 1960s. It was based on the ideals of social equality and the breakdown of social stratification espoused most clearly by Anthony Crosland in his urbane vision of a social democratic utopia of pavement cafés and cultured citizens. In the optimism of the 1950s and 60s, decades of full employment and underpinned by the 'white heat of technology', such a vision seemed quite practicable.[6] And there were many following in Crosland's footsteps, such as Roy Hattersley who continued to defend the ideals of equality in the more straitened circumstances of the 1970s and 80s, unfalteringly believing in uniform comprehensive education and universal welfare provision. Equality rather than 'choice' or freedom was the dominant value of welfare socialism. Many old believers soon discovered that there was little space for them in the New Labour party.

The welfare consensus
Many Christians in post-war Europe generally accepted the idea of social equality and welfare: a strongly regulated economy would ensure redistribution and the alleviation of want and hardship.

Where once this might have seemed dangerously leftist, from at least as early as the 1940s there was a virtually universal belief in the responsibilities of the state for the welfare of its citizens. Such ideas were popularised most effectively by William Temple, the great wartime archbishop of Canterbury, who wrote his Penguin special, *Christianity and Social Order*, in his last months as archbishop of York, publishing it in 1942 soon after his elevation to Canterbury.[7] It is a brief book which in many ways is an effort to synthesise R. H. Tawney's Christian socialism with Keynesian economics. Especially given its length it is a wide-ranging book and it quickly became a best-seller: this was principally because it was a book about the future published in some of the darkest days of the second world war. Its calls for freedom from want and an equal share for all in the resources of the country resonated with many people who were capable of looking beyond the exigencies of the national crisis.

For William Temple government existed to ensure that all families were adequately housed, that children had equal access to education, that there was sufficient income to maintain reasonable living conditions, that everybody should have a voice in the organisation of industry, that people should have sufficient time for leisure, and that there should be freedom of worship, speech and association.[8] At a practical level these proposals were to be carried out by means of high rates of taxation on unearned income, the reform and nationalisation of the banking system, and more down to earth measures like free school milk and school lunches. To co-ordinate the activities within what was called the 'welfare state',[9] planning was to be undertaken at a national level through something akin to what became known in later years as quangos (about which I will say much more in Chapter 3). Indeed, Temple claimed: 'No one doubts that in the post-war world our economic life must be "planned" in a way and to an extent that Mr Gladstone (for example) would have regarded, and condemned, as socialistic. The question is how the planning authority is to be constituted and through what channels it is to operate.'[10] At the end of his career Temple thus adopted a moderate form of socialism, which, while not exactly the opposite of heresy (as he had declared in 1908), was nonetheless the obvious implication of the welfare state. He thus admitted that 'in one sense we are committed to Socialism already'.[11] Although Temple was critical of some forms of communal ownership and other centralised forms of state control – and in that sense was distant from the sort of state socialism espoused by the Fabianism of the Webbs earlier in the century – he was nevertheless a typical exponent of the post-war consensus with its widespread acceptance of a form of planned egalitarianism. Such an understanding of the role of government moved beyond simple protection of the equality of opportunity towards a large-scale redistribution of income and a welfare safety-net.[12] As the war came to a close many of Temple's suggestions became commonplaces and were soon put into effect by post-war governments.

However, other perhaps more radical principles espoused by Temple – such as the organisation of industry on a guild system and increased devolution – were simply not discussed. This was perhaps because they were difficult to reconcile with the centralised planning which had been so essential to the command economy during the war. Thus, although in *Christianity and Social Order* Temple spends some time talking of intermediate organisations in which to realise his ideals of social fellowship,[13] and also offering a model for some form of industrial democracy, the lasting impact of his book was in providing the basis for a rights-based universal welfare system. Throughout his life Temple clamoured for a balance between the social whole and the demands of the human personality: his best-selling book again pointed to the need to find true fulfilment only in relation to society. Indeed, intermediate institutions like the 'family', schools and youth organisations were perceived to function as bearers of community, as upholders of the values of fellowship, on which flourishing human life was established. Here there are even strands of New Labour's ideal of the community in Temple's thought.[14]

The values of industrial democracy and intermediate organisations, however, are not always easy to reconcile with that other aspect of the welfare consensus, the cult of the expert. However much there might have been a move away from the welfare consensus, New Labour has retained this one crucial aspect of Old Labour thinking. Temple, like many of his contemporaries, believed wholeheartedly in central planning, which became a principal feature of the welfare state in practice.[15] This is something that has undoubtedly increased in recent years, despite the rhetoric (as I will show in Chapter 3). In William Temple's thought, as in the later history of the welfare state, great scope was given to the 'expert' who was to be called on to manage the economy and ensure that everything was done efficiently.[16] While New Labour might have been deeply critical in its rhetoric of big government and of state regulation, and although it adopted something of the Tory rhetoric of the so-called autonomy of the market, in practice it has entrusted many of the tasks of government to 'depoliticised' executive agencies in the name of efficiency and planning. The role of the expert threatens to depoliticise politics altogether.

The successes of the welfare state can hardly be denied: freedom from want and utter poverty is a great achievement of post-war governments. Yet, it seems to me, there is something inherently problematic in transferring so much decision-making authority to the realm of government. The government becomes fundamentally detached from the governed. The state becomes the provider and the manager, leading to all the problems of large-scale bureaucracy and alienation from decision-making that go along with its adoption of this role. Participatory groups (like friendly societies, trade unions and churches) are given less and less to do as the state controls all decisions. Intermediate societies with real decision-making powers beyond the control of government hardly exist.

To my mind there remains the niggling doubt that, by maintaining a notion of social structure in which the state is a divinely appointed 'order of creation' and a great manager of the economy and welfare, Temple placed far too much emphasis on the relatively transient entity of the nation state. Indeed, at one point he could write (admittedly as a very young man) that 'a man has no right to have his talents developed apart from his intention to devote them to the state. . . . Man is essentially and before all else a member of the state.'[17] A welfare state might be a benevolent kind of state, at least when compared to the 'power-state' which, on Temple's analysis, had been responsible for the first world war,[18] but it was still a state determining its citizens' welfare (even if, on Temple's model, it was always a servant of its members). In the end, however, this means that there are few limits on the legitimacy of the state's sovereignty.

When the state is elevated into an order of creation (which means little more than saying it is God-given) it becomes a necessary part of nature: it is not reformable by any human act but is a divinely appointed organ of order. All the Christian can do is to ensure that the state behaves morally: he or she can never question its legitimacy. How the state can be controlled becomes an ever more pressing issue, and it is something perceived by many politicians from across the political spectrum. As the next chapter will show, much of the New Labour language of community has been devoted to addressing this problem of the need for participation and face-to-face communities. However, the fundamental weakness in such thinking has been the absence of any serious reassessment of the role of the state and the concept of sovereignty. Few have seriously challenged the legitimacy of the nation state.

A second problem emerges from the method adopted by Temple and many later Christian socialists and social thinkers. A good example of such a thinker was Ronald Preston, one of the leading English writers on the relationship of Christianity and political economy. His distrust of ecclesiastical amateurism meant that he counselled the church to trust those and only those who were experts in their fields. The need for careful planning and management meant that the execution of political and economic decisions became the preserve of the expert. Consequently churches and other voluntary groups were not the primary agents of welfare, nor even of socialisation, but were to be understood simply as more or less prophetic institutions helping to shape public policy. This can imply an almost complete separation of the realm of political morality from the sphere of practical expertise (about which I will say a great deal more in Chapter 3). The survival of the managerialist ethos of the welfare state, which has now seemingly been applied to all corners of life, serves to bolster the authority of a target-setting state in which there is little space for individual flourishing. Community and management are two ideas which are uncomfortable bedfellows – but both seem to flow from the strange amalgam of ideas that has been embraced by New Labour. These form the themes of the next two chapters.

CHAPTER 2

Community

When I was growing up in a new town in south-east Essex I remember attending lots of functions in community centres. These ranged from children's parties organised by the Young Wives, to various concerts and fairs. It never occurred to me to ask what the community was that the community centre was supposed to be serving. Thinking back from a distance it is clear that the construction of community centres was a deliberate effort by the planners to foster some sense of community among displaced populations – in this case large numbers of Londoners, including my own parents, who had moved out of London after the war. However desirable new, cheap owner-occupied housing might be, especially when compared with the low-quality accommodation available in post-war London, something of the community spirit of the original locality was always lost. I experienced cockney knees-ups only when going to London for various family occasions. And later, from my parents and grandparents I heard much about a life that revolved around a few streets where everybody knew everybody else and where whole extended families decamped to the hop-fields of north-east Kent as a substitute for a summer holiday. While my family may not have been in London for long, having only gone there in the late nineteenth century from Northampton, they soon considered themselves Londoners and felt they belonged to that city. In south-east Essex the electrification of the railway to Southend-on-Sea and the ease of commuting drew many out of their old communities. If there was to be a community in that kind of new-town environment it would be quite different from those traditional communities based on the extended families that had been left behind. And such new communities were presumably to be fostered by the community centres.

I suppose that as a child I was unconsciously experiencing some-

thing of the great sociological problem of the nineteenth and twentieth century which was analysed by a whole range of sociologists
in terms of the move from community to society, and most clearly
enunciated by the German social theorist Ferdinand Tönnies at the
end of the nineteenth century.[1] 'Community', the name given to
small-scale face-to-face communities, made way for 'society', the
name given to the kind of social grouping where people lacked the
networks of exchange that had characterised the more traditional
societies of the past. The problem for so many planners was how
to organise modern society so that the values of community, of
mutual support and care, might continue to flourish. This same
clamour after a sense of belonging against the apparent aimless-
ness and individualism that characterise modern society is
undoubtedly behind much of the language of something called 'the
value of community' in the rhetoric of New Labour and other
Third Way parties across the world.[2] What is distinctive about Tony
Blair is his effort to locate the values of community in a specifically
Christian tradition.

Tony Blair and the values of community

Reflecting on the tenth anniversary of the publication of the
Church of England's influential *Faith in the City* report in a speech
given in Southwark Cathedral in 1996, Tony Blair charted the
changes that had taken place in British society during the previous
decade. Most important, he felt, was the collapse of 'community':
the old stable working-class communities which had provided the
backbone for the old Labour Party had collapsed as the heavy
industries had declined. The great northern towns like Sheffield or
Bradford, centred as they were on single industries, had lost the
major sources of employment upon which communities were
focused. Most painfully, throughout the 1980s mining villages had
been destroyed with nothing to replace them. Alongside this, the
pattern of manufacturing had changed: large employers like textile
mills or steel factories had made way for smaller high-tech industries or new low-wage employers such as call centres.

However, for Tony Blair, perhaps more important than the loss of
jobs and income was the moral effect of the loss of heavy industry.
A counterpart to the collapse of traditional communities was
that the values of decency and tolerance, which had knit people
together in a close moral union, were being spurned. In this

situation of moral collapse, he contended, new communities had to be reinvented before it was too late and before moral anarchy intervened. Like many others in church and society he pointed to the social nature of human beings who worked best in a team. In his Southwark Cathedral speech he claimed: 'We are social beings, nurtured in families and communities and human only because we develop the moral power of personal responsibility for ourselves and each other. Britain is simply stronger as a team than as a collection of selfish players.'[3] Developing this sporting metaphor into military language later in the speech, he declared war on 'exclusion and a determination to extend opportunity to all'.[4] The war, he continued, would not be easy to win and everybody needed to arm themselves for the fight. He concluded his speech by referring to William Temple's Malvern Declaration of 1941, where the archbishop had claimed that, in the future, all people would 'have an opportunity to become the best of which they are capable and shall find in the prosecution of their daily tasks fulfilment and not frustration of their human nature'. And to this Blair added his own gloss: 'To realise the view of human nature I have spelt out here is a challenge to all of us. On our own, we will never solve it. As one nation, together, we can.'[5] There is here a high rhetorical, almost Churchillian tone: warfare and common cause against the menace of poverty, exclusion and individualism. It was through community that one was to be armed for the future battle.

The theme of a new community founded on a shared moral vision has been the *leitmotif* of Blair's political thinking. Recognising that people no longer desired an 'overbearing' state, he claimed in a lecture in 1995 that they 'don't want to live in a vacuum either'. 'It is', he went on,

> in the search for this different, reconstructed, relationship between individual and society that ideas about 'community' are found. 'Community' implies a recognition of interdependence, but not overweening government power. It accepts that we are better equipped to meet the forces of change and insecurity through working together. It provides a basis for the elements of our character that are cooperative as well as competitive, as part of a more enlightened view of self-interest.[6]

On this analysis 'community' (a word that seems to invite inverted commas) provides the panacea for social fragmentation and the breakdown of traditional values. 'Community' offers the remedy for the decline of religion and morality which has led to a perceived increase in crime and anarchy on the streets.[7] If people knew their neighbours and cared for them – presumably even those people without a secure job or much hope for the future – then moral chaos would be overcome in a new moral order.

As it prepared for power and in its first years of office, so the notion of a new public interest, or a new moral community, became the heart of the New Labour programme and dominated its rhetoric. 'Community', according to Blair, 'is not some piece of nostalgia. It means what we share. It means working together. It is about how we treat each other.'[8] It was a vision of mutual responsibilities and sharing in which 'the individual does best in a strong and decent community of people, with principles and standards and common aims and values. It is social-ism.'[9] It was only through the balancing of the individual with the needs of society that a new community could be forged. Blair had written something similar as early as 1991 in *Marxism Today*:

> We must fashion a modern view of society which recognises the vested interests of both market and state and articulates a new over-arching concept of the public interest standing up for the individual against . . . vested interests. This requires a new political settlement between individual and society, a bargain between the two which determines rights and obligations of both sides. The notion of a modern view of society as the driving force behind the freedom of the individual is in truth the implicit governing philosophy of today's Labour Party.[10]

In policy terms the Labour government has focused its anti-poverty strategy on what is called New Deals for Communities – partnership is the key concept as local and national government seek to rebuild community in deprived areas.

Christianity, Blair and community

Blair's 'modern view of society' with its 'new over-arching concept of the public interest' embodied in the values of community has, he claims, strong Christian roots. It certainly has something in common with William Temple's headmasterly religion – the parallels with some of Temple's personalist 'Common Good' rhetoric are striking.[11] Blair, however, does not trace the roots of his communitarianism to Temple but claims to have been influenced by the writings of the Scottish Quaker moral philosopher, John Macmurray, whom he discovered at St John's College, Oxford under the guidance of the radical Australian priest, Peter Thomson. And in Blair's speeches there is undoubtedly a similarity to Macmurray. The philosopher could write, for instance, that

> we become persons in community, in virtue of our rela-
> tions to others. Human life is *inherently* a common life.
> Our ability to form individual purposes is itself a func-
> tion of this common life. . . . It is our nature; and in
> sharing a common life we are simply being ourselves by
> realizing our nature. Community is prior to society.[12]

On Blair's own account, this recognition that persons flourish only in community led him to change what he claimed was his adolescent and public-school understanding of Christianity (presumably first acquired as a chorister at Durham Cathedral) for something more profound: 'Religion became less of a personal relationship with God. I began to see it in a much more social context.' Indeed, the guiding question ever since his student days was, he suggested, how to put the idea of community into practice.[13]

Blair's conversion to the notion that persons flourish only in relationship led him to change his views. His thinking was based on a strong sense of duty and responsibility as the moral requirements for community. Here again there may be a similarity with William Temple and the other Idealists of the turn of the twentieth century – their experience of community in the very distinctive environment of an Oxford college shaped their whole approach to social thought. A socially conservative institution (in Blair's case the richest college in Oxford) provided him with a set of rules to apply more universally, but it is not clear precisely how the porters and college servants were to be part of the community, except perhaps through a highly developed sense of deference and duty.

The requirements for living in community are underpinned by acceptance of a universal set of rules which impose order on chaos. Thus Blair wrote:

All over the Western world, people are searching for a new political settlement which starts with the individual but sets him or her within the wider society. . . . People need rules which we all stand by, fixed points of agreement which impose order on chaos. . . . Duty is the cornerstone of a decent society. It recognises more than self. It defines the context in which rights are given. It is personal; but it is also owed to society. Respect for others – responsibility to them – is an essential prerequisite of a strong and active community.[14]

It is notable, however, that Blair has little to say about the source and content of these universal rules. Like Temple, he may have simply assumed that they were God-given and thus the same for everybody. There is indeed a hint of this in his writings: occasionally the concept of duty is invested with religious meaning. In an interview in the *Sunday Telegraph* in 1996 Blair claimed in one of his few openly Christian statements: 'It is from a sense of individual duty that we connect the greater good and the interests of the community – a principle the Church celebrates in the sacrament of communion.'[15] Underlying what he has to say about community is the Christian concept of the common good.

It is well known that Tony Blair is a practising member of the Church of England and has even attended Roman Catholic churches with his wife, Cherie Booth, a practising Roman Catholic. His children have been to Catholic schools with high academic (and traditional moral) standards. While publicly he may not wear his Christianity on his sleeve, he has frequently hinted at the Christian background to his thinking. His most lengthy discussion of the religious roots of his thought was given in a speech to Hans Küng's Global Ethics Foundation at Tübingen in Germany in the summer of 2000. Here he offered one of the clearest examples of what he understood by the value of community and its connections with Christianity. Although reports of the speech in the British press concentrated solely on his somewhat impractical solutions to Saturday night drunkenness, where he suggested that hooligans might be marched to cashpoints to pay on-the-spot fines, there is much else that was of interest in the speech and which emphasises the religious aspects of Blair's thinking. It also says something about where his universal rules come from.

Dealing with the conflict between the old and the new, he suggested that the resolution 'lies in applying traditional values to the modern world; to leave outdated attitudes behind; but rediscover the essence of traditional values and then let them guide us in managing change'. And then he adds, in an interesting if rather loose phrase: 'The theologians among you will say it is reuniting faith and reason.'[16] Here Blairism becomes a form of relatively conservative contextual theology: first, work out the unchanging essence of these so-called traditional values (which he goes on to enunciate as 'the modern idea of community' or 'the belief in the equal worth of all'); second, analyse the changed context (which he sees as that of a modern global economy which requires careful management); and finally, apply the ideas in the particular context. It is important to note that, for Blair, values are a matter of faith and not reason – reason's job lies solely in the application of the values of faith. Presumably, although Blair does not say as much, those who have no faith will have no values, which, it has to be admitted, is a rather disturbing thought (and which might explain his somewhat counter-cultural commitment to faith-based schools).

Further on in his speech, Blair distances himself from what he considers to be the failings of liberalism with its commitment to universal rights. Communities, he claims, are not solely to be shaped through the liberal – by which presumably he means rational and universalisable – language of rights and equality. Instead – and here he turns more Calvinist as he uses the language of covenant – Blair claims that

> you can't build a community on opportunity or rights alone. They need to be matched by responsibility and duty. That is the bargain or covenant at the heart of modern civil society. Frankly, I don't think you can make the case for Government, for spending taxpayers' money on public services or social exclusion – in other words for acting as a community – without this covenant of opportunities and responsibilities together.

And soon afterwards he returns to the familiar theme of a 'civil society of rules and order. . . . We have taken our traditional values of respect for others and solidarity, we have accepted the need for Government action, but are re-casting both values and role of Government to meet the challenge of a changing world.'

Here one can perhaps imagine a twenty-first-century Calvin marching a Genevan hooligan to a cashpoint to pay his debts to the community. What will happen to those who refuse their duties or responsibilities Blair does not say – presumably they deserve nothing in that they contribute nothing. Exile, exclusion or even execution would have been the answers of the past (and they might have worked quite well in a city-state). Moral ostracism or labelling people as scroungers would be the twenty-first-century equivalent. Blair's civil society of rules and order might offer a more benign solution than Calvin's Geneva, but there is little in the rhetoric about unconditional love for all, even those who contribute nothing. One might encourage them to participate in society, and one might increase their stake in decision-making (as I will suggest in the final chapter), but whether one should *force* them into the application of 'traditional values' (for which the term 'common good' is often a useful cipher) is altogether another question. Rights language may not be quite as redundant as Blair suggests. It may well help to protect pluralism and difference between people, which in the end might be as important as cultivating a 'community' based on responsibilities and duties, or enforcing the 'common good'.

Tony Blair concluded his speech in Tübingen by echoing Hans Küng's Global Ethic project itself. Here he turns to the language of 'globalisation' (another vague word with a whole host of different meanings). He sees an increasingly global village as one demanding a universalist ethic of peace and understanding. In this, the religions are to play their role by ensuring that values are upheld. Again, he suggests, 'faith and reason are not opponents but partners'. At this point, however, the rhetoric of 'community' expands in scope as Blair adopts language almost reminiscent of John Hick, one of the leading theorists of a so-called pluralist theology of the non-Christian religions:

> Our global community is like a tapestry; individual threads at its back; an intelligible picture at its front. All our faiths make up our global community, but they are all different ways of pondering the same fundamental question; the nature of existence. If it is true that it is only by clear commitment to shared values that we survive and prosper in a world of change, then surely religious faith

has its own part to play in deepening such commitment. What is faith but belief in something bigger than self? What is the idea of community but the national acknowledgement of our own interdependence? In truth, faith is reason's ally. . . . Religions can help to make our communities – communities of values. The inevitability of globalisation demands a parallel globalisation of our best ethical values; not a distilling or unnecessary uniformity of the rich values that make up our communities of faith. But the basic premises of our faiths; solidarity; justice; peace and the dignity of the human person are what we need in the age of globalisation.

Religion thus becomes an ally in the international search for harmony and co-operation: commonalities rather than differences between religions become the source for the new global ethic. Blair's agenda again becomes clear: the overarching religious and moral good of something called 'community' shapes values not merely in Britain but throughout the world. And furthermore, the underpinning of community through the maintenance of traditional values becomes the shared characteristic of all the great religions.

To emphasise this point, Blair concludes his speech with some rather purple language: 'Community is where they know your name; and where they miss you if you're not there. Community is society with a human face.' And most crucially it is the churches and other religious groups that are agents of such community:

Wherever you find a group that has managed to break free of the encircling bonds of poverty and deprivation, there you will invariably find strong families, associations and communities of faith. So my argument to you is that traditional values and change are not enemies but friends – because it is precisely at the epicentre of change that we need the human foundations of stability. . . . When we know we are not alone, we can face the future without fear. It is community that allows us to do so. It is values that sustain communities. And it is in a new world, global values, reaching out beyond national frontiers and ideological horizons, that will guide us to our destination: a more peaceful, secure and prosperous world for all.

It thus seems that communities are the panacea for all the problems facing the modern world – they provide the 'epicentres' of stability within the flux of change.

The Blairite irony

What is conspicuously lacking in this extraordinary elevation of the values of community in virtually every prime ministerial speech since 1997 is any reference to the traditional forms of workplace community on which the Labour Party was established. Whereas the primary agency of community formation in the early years of the Labour Party was the trade union understood usually as a participatory, even church-like, work-based institution, communities are now restricted in the new rhetoric to the public and voluntary sphere that exists between state, workplace and individual. In place of the trades unions and co-operatives come other voluntary organisations, especially faith-based groups, which exist to foster values of community and solidarity. Perhaps ironically, faith communities, most of which have seen an enormous decline in the past twenty years, are given the responsibility for providing society with values. Faith – at least in its traditional Christian forms – seems to be required for politics at precisely the same time that it is becoming ever more marginal to British society.

It is perhaps surprising that there is no hint in Blair's speeches of the fact that Christianity is declining exponentially in Britain. Indeed, irony is not a strong component of the Blairite rhetoric. More and more weight is placed on the epicentres of stability at precisely the time that they are threatened with virtual non-existence. To stretch the metaphor: the churches simply do not cause many earthquakes any longer. In Britain, church membership and practice have halved in forty years: in 1960 there were 190,713 confirmations in the Church of England; in 1980 this had fallen to 97,620 and by 1997 it was a mere 40,881. Other Christian denominations have followed much the same pattern of decline. Some have fared even worse, as with the United Reformed Church. Dechristianisation seems to be growing ever more rapidly: in this situation Christianity becomes a lifestyle choice rather than something that is simply the warp and weft of British society. Although, according to the 2001 census, 70 per cent of the British still regard themselves as Christians, the sense in which this

Christianity results in action or associates with the Christian churches is not at all obvious.

Churches will no doubt continue to exist for their adherents for a long time yet, but it is impossible to re-create the Christian nation: the culture of Christianity has vanished. Sunday schools and the popular religious attitudes they helped instil have all but disappeared. As many commentators have shown, Christianity, where it continues to exist, is part of the private discourse rather than a 'publicly available background'. It has stopped effecting change in most individuals, and in turn will stop changing society at least explicitly – in response, British culture, according to Callum Brown's bleak view, is 'pioneering new discursive territory',[17] which is not necessarily religious at all. Where the maintenance of values requires faith (as Blair seems to believe) then the future of values looks decidedly fragile and unstable. To a greater or lesser extent something similar is true for most of Europe.[18] In some Catholic countries the figures indicate almost complete collapse. In France, for instance, the average age of Catholic clergy was 66 in 1989 and is still rising. Similarly the figure for baptisms, which indicates nominal membership, has fallen from 92 per cent in 1958 to 58 per cent in 1993. Seeing values as a matter of faith means that the survival of European morality is itself altogether a risky business.

Community and values

Of course, Tony Blair is not alone in his call for revitalised communities, and in his use of the rhetoric of unity and solidarity. The clamour for community goes back a long way and is shared by many thinkers from a variety of backgrounds, many of them quite unreligious and not demanding the levels of commitment to faith that Blair's thought appears to require. Although they may not be overtly religious, however, many seem to share his notion of the need for a universal moral purpose. Raymond Plant, writing as long ago as 1984, for instance, observed that 'we lack a rich conception of political community, and with it a sense of membership and citizenship, and therefore of the way in which the state could embody the moral purpose of community'.[19] For socialists of different hues this clamour can be seen to be a return to the old French revolutionary ideal of fraternity against the excessive individualism of modern society. There are evident parallels with the thought of Émile Durkheim, the great French sociologist, and the earlier eccentric socialist Henri de Saint-Simon, both of whom clamoured for new forms of community in complex industrial society. Indeed, as I hinted in the opening section of this chapter, perhaps the greatest sociological question of the nineteenth and twentieth century was this: how is it possible to re-create an ethics of communal involvement and participation in a fragmented society? How can we reinvent communities in our contemporary world which function like the small-scale face-to-face communities of the past?

At the same time, an emphasis on community has been seen as an answer to the social levelling of state-imposed egalitarianism, which is the by-product of the excessive regulation of the welfare state and its top-downwards model of socialism. In such a situation people lack any sense of belonging and control, becoming instead passive recipients of state handouts and diktats. The political historian David Marquand has summarised this problem in terms of the loss of freedom:

> The great engine of social democratic redistribution has always been tax-financed public expenditure . . . but if the state takes my money away from me to give it to some-one else, my freedom is thereby diminished. If those to whom it is given receive it in the form of cash, which they can spend as they like, and if there are a lot of them and only a few of me, there may well be a net gain in freedom. If they receive it in the form of services, in the direction of which they have no say and over the alloca-tion of which they have no control, there will be no gain in freedom, though there may still be a gain in equality.[20]

Consequently, against the socialist experiments of the past, which have so often led to state control and a liberty-denying depen-dency on welfare, many thinkers, including Tony Blair and his New Labour ideologues, have sought what they claim to be new values, which they see as able to protect the values of both community or fraternity and personal freedom. Marquand himself calls this 'civic republicanism'[21] which he sees as promoting communal ideas against the increasing fragmentation of modern (or perhaps more properly post-modern) society with its lack of any overarching consensus ('metanarrative'). In short, according to Marquand,

the values of community and fellowship speak as loudly . . .
to the late twentieth century as to earlier periods. Indeed,
in some respects they are more pertinent . . . than they used
to be. . . . The old communalism is fading, and no one has
yet found a new communalism to replace it. . . . Perhaps the
central question for our time is whether insight and ethic
can be brought together in a new project with some pur-
chase on social reality.[22]

In recent years, however, Marquand has become far more aware of
the decline of the public sphere and the civic ideal itself.[23]

Other thinkers of a more Romantic persuasion are equally
enamoured of the idea of community. Some see the project as a
creative rearticulation of ideas developed in the past which had
long been forgotten. For some, William Morris, one of the first
socialist critics of the disintegrating effects of capitalism in the
second half of the nineteenth century, has become the prophet of
small-scale communities relevant for the present day.[24] It must be
said, however, that concrete solutions are as decidedly lacking in
these thinkers as they were for Morris: history is littered with failed
experiments in utopian community.[25]

The international dimension: the Third Way
It is also important to note that the clamour for community as a
solution to the perceived fragmentation of modern society is not
unique to Britain, but has been adopted in progressive politics
around the world. It has often been called 'Third Way' politics since
it moves beyond the individualism of unbridled capitalism and the
oppressive bureaucracy of state socialism. In his opening speech to
the London Conference on Progressive Governance in July 2003
Blair outlined this clearly. Fundamental to Third Way politics, he
said,

> is the re-casting of the relationship between citizen and
> state; to one that is neither dependency; nor abandon-
> ment; but a partnership between the two based on
> mutual rights and responsibilities to provide opportunity
> and security for all in the face of globalization. A rela-
> tionship of dependency is a welfare state that simply gives
> to its recipients; who expect to be given to and who get
> what is given. It tends to be monolithic and passive.

Abandonment is where much of the right want to go, where, in an increasingly insecure world, people sink or swim according to their own devices.[26]

Third Way politics moved beyond left and right in a new partnership.

The meeting of the Conference on Progressive Governance held in Berlin three years earlier in June 2000 provides a good illustration of the international dimension of this form of politics. After President Clinton's closing speech a journalist asked him why he had not used the term 'Third Way'. Was this, the journalist wondered, a turning point? The President hoped not and went on to defend the idea:

> That term, the Third Way, is fairly closely identified with our administration and with what Prime Minister Blair has done in Great Britain. And I think this idea of progressive governance is perhaps less of a political slogan and more of a description of what it is we're all trying to do. We don't believe in just laissez faire economics, but we don't believe that government alone can solve these problems or ignore the importance of economic performance. So what we want is progressive governance to deal with the opportunities and challenges that are out there.

There were also some things which even governments could not solve, but which required better management. Besides, the President continued: 'I like the Third Way because it's sort of easy to remember.' At this point, perhaps to prevent further degeneration in the intellectual level of debate, the German Chancellor Gerhard Schröder intervened to explain the British Prime Minister's absence, for which, he claimed, there was a very good reason: 'a baby has just been born. And that's all, that's the whole story.' The President, however, could not resist a witty quip: 'Progressive governance and the Third Way are pro-family.'[27]

This quip, however, contains rather more substance than the President might have realised. At its heart, the so-called Third Way, just like Tony Blair's emphasis on community, is an odd blend of the modern and the traditional. A fixation on being utterly up to date, with globalisation, with the knowledge economy and expertise in management,[28] goes hand in hand with the revival of traditional values, in particular those of the community and family. In its own self-perception, the Third Way seeks to be something of a blend of the old and the new; modern managed economics leaps into bed with family and communitarian values, which are usually little more than those of good old-fashioned decency and courtesy: they can sometimes be rather unlikely partners.

Tony Blair repeated this point to a very different audience in the summer of 2000. In his disastrously received speech to the fiercely non-political National Federation of Women's Institutes he claimed: 'The way we do [politics] is to combine the old and the new, traditional British values of responsibility and respect for others; with a new agenda of opportunity for all in a changing world.'[29] In this sort of thinking, there is an evident concern with the re-moralisation of politics, perhaps most clearly expressed by Anthony Giddens in his short Third Way manifesto.[30] Giddens, who is Director of the London School of Economics, has become something of a Blairite guru and court philosopher to New Labour. In a relatively populist fashion he maintains that the Third Way steers between the laissez-faire economics of Thatcherism and the old socialist values of universal welfare provision by a bureaucratic state. It aims to achieve this by rediscovering the values of community and mutual responsibility.

Christianity, community and the Third Way

Since 11 September 2001 and the devastation of the World Trade Center, the language of community has continued unabated, but with an ever greater emphasis on fostering relationships between the nations (as was noted, for instance, by Jack Straw, the Foreign Secretary, in his Mansion House speech of April 2002). The language of community knows no national boundaries. Shortly after the September events Tony Blair said to the Labour Party Conference in October 2001: 'The critics will say: but how can the world be a community? Nations act in their own self-interest. Of course they do. But what is the lesson of the financial markets, climate change, international terrorism, nuclear proliferation or world trade? It is that our self-interest and our mutual interests are today inextricably woven together.' The way out of all these problems is through what he calls the 'power of community'. Indeed, he claims, 'Our values are the right ones for this age: the power of community, solidarity, the collective ability to further the individual's interests.' Ideology might be dead, but the values of community live on, a theme which is repeated throughout the speech. Blair concluded: 'For those people who lost their lives on September 11 and those that mourn them; now is the time for the strength to build that community. Let that be their memorial.'[31] Who will decide on precisely what the values of community consist of is left unsaid.

A similar theme has been repeated in Blair's more recent speeches. For instance, in his speech to the Scottish Labour Party Conference in February 2002, he talks about government policy as

> applying our traditional values of community and social justice, opportunity for all, to the modern world. . . . The central insight of New Labour today is that we live in an inter-dependent world, where the interests of society and the individuals within it coincide. A stronger community where we use the talents of all the people within it, makes all more prosperous.[32]

Again he concludes with the values of community, this time listed as a set of aphorisms, which though remarkably short on content, are nevertheless terribly British:

> Our policies may change but our values remain the same. Social justice. Opportunity for all. Community. The belief that we are a community of people, and a community of nations. Strong together. Achieving more together than we can alone. These are values that every Labour leader from Keir Hardie onwards would recognise. Scottish values. British values. Labour values. Values that are worth fighting for. Values that will sustain us as we continue our journey of change and deliver the Britain that we promised, the Britain the people want, the Britain the world needs.

There is indeed little that the values of community (and its synonyms) cannot achieve. As Blair put it at the 2002 Labour Party Conference:

> The key characteristic of today's world is interdependence. Your problem becomes my problem. They have to

be tackled collectively. . . . Interdependence is the core
reality of the modern world. It is revolutionising our idea
of national interest. It is forcing us to locate that interest
in the wider international community. It is making solidarity – a great social democratic ideal – our route to
practical survival. Partnership is statesmanship for the 21st
Century.

At the local level this is reflected in the claim that the 'modern
Welfare State must be active, not passive, put partnership in place of
paternalism. That's what a modern civic society, with reformed
public services and welfare can do.' Blair moves on to a call to
involvement in community for anybody interested in a 'healthy
democracy', and ends with a slogan: 'At our best when at our
boldest.'[33]

All in all, a great deal is invested in the values of community: but
there are many questions that are left unanswered. Most obviously,
so little is actually said about exactly what constitutes a community, that this urgently needs clarification. Similarly, how precisely
the community is to function and what its role should be in relation to national and local politics are simply never discussed. And
even more importantly, how local and national communities relate
to those outside is seldom tackled: there is lots of talk about
partnership but little about how to achieve it. Without some analysis of the relationships between communities and who precisely is
a member of community, the language of community will remain
a fairly empty piece of vague rhetoric.

Consequently, several problems emerge which urgently require
solutions: who is to arbitrate between communities when they disagree, and on what will they base their criteria? Unless everybody
agrees on a common good then such criteria will always be open
to question. As a result we are immediately forced into a detailed
discussion of political authority and the related concept of
sovereignty. Because so much is invested in the notion of community, it seems imperative to flesh out its meaning and the authority
structures it implies in as much detail as possible. Since the
rhetoric holds that the traditional values represented by the concept
of community require some sort of faith, the discussion will necessarily address the theology of sovereignty. The last two chapters of
this book will be devoted to that task.

However, I will conclude this chapter as I started, with a personal reflection. For the past twelve years I have lived in a Christian community: I have shared the daily office twice a day with those training for ministry in the Church of England. I have eaten many of my meals in a common dining hall, and I have got to know people in considerable depth. There may be something of a common aim and a common set of values and it is undoubtedly a community that is sustained by a faith in a fairly traditional set of values. For much of the time, life together in community is both rewarding and stimulating. But at times it is not: not surprisingly, given that people are living a tiring and fairly intense life cheek by jowl, there are frequent conflicts. And it is often through that conflict that the community changes.

What unites the visions of community promoted by the politicians and their ideologues is the need to foster a form of fraternity in which there will be shared objectives and a harmonious way of life. But fraternity is a hard-won value which needs to be worked at: the common good, if it ever emerges, is usually brought about through very real conflict. If communities are also about conflict then they may well be rather more unsettling than many have hitherto believed. Communities may be important to overcome something of the fragmentation of the modern world, but they will often be fragmented themselves. This, I will suggest, has been more or less overlooked by the New Labour ideologues. Indeed, it may well be that Anthony Crosland's superficial vision of communities of cappuccino drinkers enjoying a good chat, or the like-minded community of the Delia Smith dinner party, have been rather more influential on New Labour thinking than one might have initially thought. Yet this form of community is far from typical: instead, communities in the real world (or at least a world more real than Islington) are often made up of people who do not particularly like one another and who would not choose to be together, but who need ways of coming to decisions and of living together even when they do not share much of what one would call a common good. And, even more disturbingly, sometimes where they do unite around a common good it might well be purchased at the expense of somebody else's good. Nothing unites a community more than a common enemy: sadly the past two years, with the invasion of Iraq and the resulting re-election of President George W. Bush in November 2004, have proved this point once again.

CHAPTER 3

Management

It is probably not a nice thing to be a manager: managers do not get a good press. This seems to be especially true for managers in the public sector where red tape is seen as the leading vice. Health service managers in particular come in for a great deal of stick – some of the rhetoric from all the political parties seems to suggest that hospitals will simply manage themselves if nurses and doctors (almost always immune from criticism) are allowed to make clinical judgements unfettered by bureaucracy. What is conveniently forgotten is the fact that any publicly funded health service will inevitably require judgements to be made between scarce resources: there will be inevitable compromises. This means that some sort of management of resource allocation is necessary and unavoidable. The question remains, however, as to precisely what sort of management is best, and how much is needed. Although the word may not feature as frequently as the catch-all buzzword of community, the notion of efficient and accountable management has become the other leading value of New Labour. I will suggest in this chapter that it has been a highly impressive political sleight of hand, allowing the New Labour government to become the most centralist government of post-war years – all in the name of efficiency, audit and accountable management.

In its period of office New Labour has become one of the most managerially inclined governments of all time. And this emphasis on management is something that transcends the divisions between Tony Blair and Gordon Brown, the Chancellor of the Exchequer: both have succeeded in elevating efficient management, particularly of the economy, into a separate order of creation which rests beyond politics. As this chapter will show, Blair and, perhaps even more importantly, Brown, have come to see management not simply as a means to an end but as an end in itself, as something

which is the principal function of good and responsible government acting in the best interests of its citizens. Perhaps most
crucially, good management is like the British weather – it simply
cannot be changed. It lies beyond the scope of the politician and
has to be left to the experts. How and why this has happened is the
subject of this chapter, which will also raise questions about how
the culture of audit threatens the very institutions it aims to regulate.

The 'quangoisation' of the state

The history of the years since 1 May 1997 is marked by the proliferation of executive agencies and other quangos: this amounts to
what might be regarded as an extraordinary depoliticisation of the
public sphere. The mode of governance has become something
indirect, often devolved to agencies and institutions which operate
at arm's length from the political (and democratic) process: everything from English Heritage to school inspection has been increasingly depoliticised, and occasionally even put in the hands of the
private sector acting as agents for the government. These agencies
are frequently guided by their own sets of values which are sometimes only very loosely under the control of the democratically
elected government, either at a national or local level. The over-
riding principle seems to be to base government on expertise,
which in turn derives from a view of the social sciences and economics as somehow autonomous and outside the sphere of value-
judgements. This means that the actions of many agencies are
beyond politics, and are best seen as specialist activities undertaken
and understood only by experts. Here New Labour thinking is
remarkably similar to the welfare thinking of the past: the
Fabianism of the Webbs and the welfare state of William Temple
both placed great trust in the expert (while never quite removing
the social sciences and economics from the sphere of political control altogether).

With New Labour, however, things have been taken still further.
This is particularly true in the realm of economics. According to
New Labour thinking, the processes of economics and management are governed by natural laws which constrain the sphere of
political activity. This is not usually quite so simplistic as Mrs
Thatcher's famous judgement that 'You can't buck the market';
nevertheless in a sense New Labour has accepted a situation in

which government responsibility for certain key areas of economic policy has been devolved to a team of experts from whom there is no escape. This in turn means that there is less and less scope for the moral and political regulation of economic and social life. One might thus ask: if economic and social activity are guided by necessary laws beyond any human control, what then is the sphere that is left for politics and morality? All that seems left for governments to do is simply to nudge the laws a little in the hope that this might steer them in the right kind of direction. If this is the case then it is crucial to ask whether government economic policy has become little more than a technical rationality devoid of ethical content. Or, to put it another way, whether crucial moral decisions are being evaded under the guise of economic neutrality.

Sometimes it almost seems as if the high-sounding values spoken of by Blair in his pronouncements on community, and his clamour for the persistence of faith to make such communities possible (as discussed at length in the last chapter), have to make way for a pure and value-free rationality in the complex economic reality of the modern world. In the cut and thrust of the real world, it appears, there is little space for values at all. It is my contention in this chapter that the place given to the technical solutions of the economist and the other experts operating in their executive agencies (and almost anything can develop into a specialism) has become so elevated that there is frequently no space left for morality and politics. We have reached the world of what might be called anti-politics. It is important to note that the cult of the apolitical expert can easily slide over into the absolutisation of the economic and managerial; and in turn it might be easy to slide over into a form of idolatry – after all, absolutes tend to be worthy of worship. This frightening cult where values are excised from all government activity, I will suggest, may have dire consequences for the future of politics. Indeed, politics might cease to exist altogether, and if that is the case, then who would try to change the world? There would be no point in martyrdom, or any other form of political activity for that matter, since values would have disappeared altogether.

'There is no alternative': redefining the political

First of all, it is important to analyse the reshaping of political discourse. The underlying question is simple but intriguing: if management is not a word to champion (unlike community), then how is it that it has featured so prominently in New Labour policy? Political rhetoric has developed into such a complex art form that it must have been a real challenge to the spin doctors to be able to contort the language of management (a 'bad' word) from negative to positive, even if the word 'management' itself has usually been avoided. But New Labour wasn't working in a vacuum. It built on the legacy of the past. Indeed, in many ways their spin doctors simply developed the sort of media-management techniques used so effectively in Downing Street during the Thatcher years. Alastair Campbell, New Labour's spin doctor *par excellence*, followed closely in the footsteps of Bernard Ingham, Mrs Thatcher's Press Secretary. Controlling the public image and public discourse has become central to modern politics. The story of the rise of managerial rhetoric presents a splendid illustration of the art of manipulation. To begin to understand how it developed, it is necessary to return to the dismal early years of Mrs Thatcher's first government of the 1980s.

What these years proved was that sometimes a firm control of political language can redefine the sphere of what counts as politics altogether. One obvious example can be used to demonstrate this. In May 1980 Margaret Thatcher, after a year in office, made her famous statement that there was simply no alternative to the strictest possible control of the money supply in economic policy. This meant that, at a stroke, it became impossible to alter economic policy through government activity. Suddenly economics, one of the main preoccupations of post-war governments, had become depoliticised; and given the primacy of economics over all other activities of government, this meant in turn that the scope for all forms of political activity was severely constrained. All the efforts by governments to control the many different aspects of macro-economic policy, which had occupied Chancellors of the Exchequer through much of the 1960s and 70s, were ruled out of court. For Mrs Thatcher these other policies were simply not genuine alternatives but denials of a fundamental truth: control of the money supply was the only policy available. It was as if by shouting loudly enough and by saying the same thing over and over again, one of her most impressive characteristics and one taken up by her disciples and publicists, Mrs Thatcher had managed to change the content of politics.

Furthermore, there was almost something of the quality of faith in her approach to economic policy. Like the trust implied by religious faith, in no sense was there any need to justify the statement – it was a truth given in the very constitution of the world. Indeed, her bold suggestion that 'There is no alternative', which made its first appearance in the *Daily Telegraph* on 22 May 1980, was used so often that it became known simply by the soubriquet 'TINA'. While there patently was an alternative, this simple statement and its constant repetition helped reshape political discourse. There was a certain incredulity among many economists – after all, quite different approaches dominated economic policy after the second world war. No fewer than 364 economists responded in a letter to *The Times*, pointing out the variety of economic options on offer. But none of this criticism mattered to the true believer. Control of the money supply was all that was possible, despite its dire economic repercussions. It had become a kind of economic fundamentalism that allowed for no criticism. Those who disagreed in the government soon found themselves isolated, or dismissed.

Because monetarism was the only possible course of action this meant that the social effects of such a policy were simply necessary evils. There was no sense in which they could be placed in the sphere of morality, since they were unavoidable consequences of the only available course of action. If unemployment had to rise because of deflationary policies, then so be it. TINA meant that economics was removed from ethics altogether. There was simply nothing else that could be done. Massive unemployment and the collapse of Britain's manufacturing base which followed the disastrous policies of the early 1980s were completely unavoidable, quite simply because the government had no choice. Mrs Thatcher's simple statement helped reshape political discourse; to use a term borrowed from W. H. Riker's book *The Art of Political Manipulation*, it was 'heresthetic'.[1] This word describes the type of political language where rhetoric moves beyond the simple art of persuasion to a complete redefinition of the terms of the political debate. 'Persuading people that it was true', writes Iain McLean, 'made it true.'[2] In Orwellian terms, Mrs Thatcher's TINA was an extraordinarily successful form of Newspeak.

The Blairite TINA

It would not be beyond the bounds of possibility to suggest that there may be something similar at work in some of the rhetoric of

New Labour. Although McLean himself does not detect any direct equivalent to TINA in more recent political rhetoric, he nevertheless recognises an important process of redefinition in New Labour of what counts as political: in this connection, the most important act of the first days of the New Labour government was the handing over to the Bank of England and its Monetary Policy Committee (MPC) of 'operational responsibility for setting interest rates to meet the Government's inflation target'.[3] In decided continuity with the Thatcherite removal of governmental responsibility for the Keynesian instruments of economic planning after 1979, Gordon Brown thus moved one step further in reducing the role of politics in economic policy. Within broad strategic parameters interest rates were put in the hands of an unelected board of experts one step removed from government. It is thus now possible for the government (and that now means any future government of whatever hue) to deny responsibility for anything (such as unemployment and crippling indebtedness) which might result from changes in interest rates: they can no longer be used as political instruments.

It is worthwhile looking in more detail at the Chancellor of the Exchequer's stated criteria for the selection of his four appointees to the MPC. Foremost among these was the notion of 'professional competence and independence'. The fact that the 'professional competence' of bankers might well be dependent on a completely different set of values from those which were supposedly upheld by New Labour's values of community was not apparently considered: professional competence was beyond morality. Similarly, political 'independence' could easily imply independence from any sense of ethical responsibility at all. However, despite the claim to independence in the MPC, there was still a firm control set by the centre: keeping to an inflation target decided by the government ruled out any other policy objectives. It became Brown's more benign equivalent of the Thatcherite TINA.

In the name of independence and expertise the government could still rule by a quasi-divine fiat, but one beyond the purview of parliament (since it had been devolved to the MPC). Somewhat cynically, it could be seen as a way of shifting the blame in the event that things went wrong – economic failures were no longer the government's fault, but were simply necessary evils imposed on economic policy by those with 'professional competence' who knew best. Writing to the Chancellor at the end of his tenure on the MPC, Willem Buiter noted the uncompromising character of the single objective, praising

> [the] transparency and openness of the arrangements and the accountability of those who participate in [the MPC]. There is now a widely-based constituency for low inflation. There is growing awareness of the sometimes uncomfortable truth, that it is through the uncompromising pursuit of macroeconomic stability for the country as a whole, that we best serve the long-term interests of all its citizens and of its diverse regions, sectors and industries.[4]

On this kind of analysis, politics was to be held at a distance from efficient economic management however uncomfortable that might be. The goals of economic efficiency were regarded as too important to be subjected to political control and were consequently handed over to the professionals but firmly steered from the centre.

Resistance is futile

It is not simply in the sphere of the economic, however, that there has been a subtle reshaping of political discourse. It can easily be shown that the redefining of the notion of accountability and political responsibility has been one of the most important characteristics of government policy since 1997: it is closely connected with a rhetoric that talks of managing the inevitable through 'expertise' and seeing the role of government in terms of audit. Tony Blair has sometimes spoken as if the modern world, with its sophisticated economic and trading relationships, is simply too powerful and too complex to be shaped by politicians. Consequently the only option for politicians is to manage the inevitable as best and as efficiently as they can. In the same speech delivered in the summer of 2000 to Hans Küng's Global Ethics Foundation where he revealed so much about his understanding of the Christian faith, Blair also interestingly redefined the boundaries for political action. At one point he reaches a set of questions which can only be described as his attempt at heresthetic redefinition:

> The change is fast and fierce, replete with opportunities and dangers. The issue is: do we shape it or does it shape

us? Do we master it, or do we let it overwhelm us? That's
the sole key to politics in the modern world: how to
manage change. Resist it: futile; let it happen: dangerous.
So – the third way – manage it. But it can't be managed
unless there are rules of management, value judgments as
to how and why we are managing it in a particular way.[5]

Blair thus suggests that the forces of change in the modern world
are so strong that there is no alternative to responsible, efficient and
careful management. It is indeed futile to resist management since
it is the only area left for the modern politician. The rather
frightening phrase 'Resistance is futile' (RIF) might even be the
Blairite equivalent of the Thatcherite TINA. Where this leaves
politicians as agents of moral change and purveyors of the common
good, which provides so much of the rest of the New Labour
rhetoric, is left unexplored. Efficient management seems a very
different value from that of building community.

In more concrete terms this fixation on the need for efficient
management has led the New Labour government to follow the
path set by its immediate predecessors in the massive growth of the
number of managerial executive agencies and other quangos which
now control vast areas of social policy. The government proudly lists
over one thousand public bodies of varying sizes and with varying
responsibilities made up of thirty thousand members, most of
whom are appointed by the government, or nominated by various
interest groups; sometimes they are even appointed by the self-
perpetuating quango itself. In many of these agencies the government's only role is in target setting, 'benchmarking' and ensuring
efficient economic implementation through constant audit.
Morality, traditional values, and even the long-standing socialist
language of liberty, fraternity and equality, make way for technical
expertise and quantifiable targets. Management becomes an
autonomous science reduced solely to the goal of economic
efficiency and virtually devoid of morality.

Christians and the future of public morality
It is precisely at this point that it becomes crucial for Christians and
others to help re-establish a proper sphere for political morality
before it is too late. The contemporary cult of the expert and
target-setter does not bode well for the long-term survival of

public institutions and political morality. Political activism becomes ever more important for the survival of democracy at precisely the point where it is under threat through the anti-politics of audit. Indeed, it is not difficult to claim that unless Christians are active in the supposedly neutral, depoliticised and consequently de-ethicised sphere of audit, then there will simply be no Christian input into politics (since in the long run there will be no politics). In turn, this might mean that Christians will be forced to argue for the very possibility of political and public morality, against the prevalent economic and managerial reductionism. And it will become more and more important to reveal the hidden values of target setting and audit.

It seems to me that the main duty for contemporary Christians, some of whom may wish to call themselves socialists, is the repoliticisation and remoralisation of economic and social life, against rule by supposedly depoliticised quangos and the reduction of ethical activity solely to the politically ineffectual realm of civil society. Here an important link emerges with themes discussed in the previous chapter: it may be that talk of the 'civil society' and all the vague 'community' language that goes along with it is little more than a mask for an unquestioning acceptance of the 'inevitable' domination of the political sphere by a de-ethicised and de-politicised economics.

Consequently, even though there may be an emphasis on 'impartiality' and openness in interest- or lobby-group representation as demonstrated by the MPC, vast areas of social policy are now controlled by appointed officials and boards answerable solely to the executive, and to neither voter, worker nor consumer.[6] All that is left in terms of democratic accountability is the blunt instrument of voting out the ruling party in the occasional general election. The so-called neutrality of the managerial process, especially when even the executive has lost control to the 'expert', makes it increasingly difficult to shape political policy. Such a situation is hardly likely to lead to high levels of participation in the decision-making process. In addition, local political control at county, district and parish level has frequently become little more than the local implementation of targets decided centrally and delegated to councils, agencies or private companies. This too amounts to a 'depoliticisation' by central government in that it allows the government to blame local councils, primary care trusts, or even private companies (like the

Criminal Records Bureau and OFSTED inspection teams) for its own failures or inadequate funding. The extraordinary levels of executive control mean that parliament (to whom the executive is at least in theory accountable) is similarly reduced in its powers of scrutiny and oversight.

Furthermore, appointed bureaucracies now control what were once self-governing and relatively democratic communities, which in turn have had to establish their own bureaucracies to implement government orders. Hitherto unmeasurable activities (like academic excellence) are now measured in terms of economic goods (publications) or various forms of 'quality' for which quantifiable criteria are given. In such a situation managerial audit directed from above has become the universal experience of public servants, even when they work in organisations, such as universities and hospitals, which have traditionally been upheld by quite different and unquantifiable sets of moral ideals and goals (like the pursuit of truth or health).[7] The Quality Assurance Agency for higher education, for instance, has a 'mission to promote public confidence that quality of provision and standards of awards in higher education are being safeguarded and enhanced'. This is executed 'by auditing the way in which each university and college manages the overall quality and standards of its provision; and by reviewing academic standards and the quality of teaching and learning in each subject area'. Universities, once essentially self-governing and accountable to teaching staff, boards of governors (which in the case of the old polytechnics usually included the local authorities) and other participatory bodies, have thereby been standardised through an audit conducted by auditors nominated by the agency itself on the advice of the institutional managers. As the common experience of those working in the university sector will testify, such a system is hardly likely to create the conditions where participation and trust might flourish. The role of the university is now to achieve the targets set by the QAA.

A similar experience can be found in many other public services: the 'political' has been deliberately removed and has been replaced with a managerialism which inevitably changes the conceptions of participation and trust in public bodies. The worker is placed at the mercy of the managers, who in turn ensure the performance of functions and targets set from outside in which they have little say and in which there is little delegation of responsibility. Trust in self-determination makes way for external managerial command where the managed lack representation in decision-making processes. The managers in turn become the tools of the regulative agencies. Morale sinks to all-time lows as Max Weber's iron cage of bureaucracy becomes an ever-present reality which stifles creativity.

This loss of democratic control and accountability helps explain the extraordinarily low levels of participation in the political process, particularly in local council elections: after all, what is the point of voting for a local council when it is principally an agency of central government with few fiscal and decision-making powers? Not surprisingly, mavericks who are prepared to criticise the central government, or even to dress up as monkeys (as was the case in Hartlepool), have been elected as local mayors. Whether the policy initiatives outlined at the 2002 Labour Party Conference which aim to redirect decision-making to the local will do much to redress this problem is questionable: no legislation has been forthcoming and there is little sign of any loosening of control.

With its lack of accountability, its detachment from local knowledge and its unwillingness to trust existing agencies, the fiasco of the Millennium Dome epitomises the failures of the managerialist state. This expensive and almost-tragic farce represented the triumphant failure of centralised planning: the managerialist state alienates those very people on whose support it claims to base its legitimacy. In his book on *Authority in the Modern State* of 1919 H. J. Laski wrote of the inherent vice of 'centralised authority', which seems to me to be equally applicable to the problems of today. The modern state, he wrote,

> is so baffled by the very vastness of its business as necessarily to be narrow and despotic and over-formal in character. It tends to substitute for a real effort to grapple with special problems an attempt to apply wide generalisations that are in fact irrelevant. It involves the decay of local energy by taking real power from its hands. It puts real responsibility in a situation where, from its very flavour of generality, an unreal responsibility is postulated. It prevents the saving grace of experiment.[8]

That amounts to a clear summary of the chief problems which led to the Millennium Dome, currently decaying unwanted in a deprived area of former Greenwich dockland.

In many ways the centralising approach seems quite out of place in the post-1989 world. The threats that helped preserve the siege mentality and a sense of national solidarity have more or less vanished. The economy cannot be contained by any theory of autarky or 'Keynesian' planning within national boundaries. Instead, transnational institutions limit the functions of the state, and globalisation transcends the confines of any national economy. In both the centralised socialism of the East and the social democracy of the West an inefficient and distant bureaucracy showed itself unable or unwilling to deliver on its promises, and all that was left in the vacuum of the post-communist world was the cement of the market, which often did little more than increase the gulf between rich and poor.[9] In such a situation, the panaceas of less secure times seemed to have reached their sell-by date. Alasdair MacIntyre has been one of the most vigorous critics of the failings of the modern nation state, which he regards as a 'dangerous and unmanageable institution, presenting itself on the one hand as a bureaucratic supplier of goods and services, which is always about to, but never actually does, give its clients value for money, and on the other as a repository of sacred values, which from time to time invite one to lay down one's life on its behalf . . . it is like being asked to die for the telephone company'.[10] With a lack of trust in central institutions, which seem to have lost their whole *raison d'être*, levels of participation in the democratic process sink ever lower, and democracy becomes often little more than a periodic plebiscite: the managerial state has succeeded in marginalising politics altogether.

More controversially, whatever their democratic claims, it can be shown with some degree of plausibility that British governments have maintained an early modern theory of sovereignty, where any alternative source of power is seen either as a threat or a concession. On such a theory, where communities begin to threaten the state, or to wield any independent power (as with trades unions in the past), then they contravene the Tudor theory of kingship which provides the foundation for the British constitution. This theory continues to inform the present government's understanding and exercise of authority through virtually unbridled executive action (admittedly implemented rather more benignly).[11] Indeed it is not completely ridiculous to see Thomas Cromwell as leader of the first quango. He was, after all, appointed by and answerable to a very powerful executive.[12] Tony Blair may be no Henry VIII, but his government still operates on a theory of sovereignty which has changed remarkably little. Executive power may no longer be justified in terms of the divine right of kings, but the idea of a managerialism that is beyond all question, least of all by the people and participants, becomes functionally equivalent to the power of the Tudor state. And although there may be less risk to one's head, it can be equally dangerous for the flourishing of the individual in society. The implications of this will be discussed more fully in the final chapter.

CHAPTER 4

Theologies of Community and Theologies of Conflict

In general, Christians (like New Labour) have tended to assume that 'community' is a good thing. For those of a theological bent, there has been a fair bit of effort spent in trying to construct a theology of community. Many have found the answer in the doctrine of the Trinity, of God as some sort of community. There is patently much that appeals in the notion of a God who is perfect communion. God becomes a picture of a harmony in whom the struggles and conflicts that characterise human life are overcome. The doctrine of God as communion (*koinonia*) provides a refuge for the beleaguered theologian struggling to apply doctrine to society: a vision of harmony and balanced relationships looks like a healthy alternative to an increasingly disordered and dysfunctional society. In this, theologians share much common ground with the ideologues of New Labour and the Third Way. Indeed, so-called 'social' doctrines of the Trinity might even be seen as New Labour-style rhetoric applied to God (although most theologians would no doubt disagree and would prefer to see things from the other direction, as the doctrine of God applied to human communities).

The Trinity and community

There is, however, nothing particularly new in this sort of theology. For instance, Conrad Noel (1869–1942), the rebellious vicar of Thaxted in Essex, tried to ground his socialist vision in the doctrine of the Trinity. The 'world-commonwealth in which the equality and justice and mercy of its divine original will be manifested'[1] with its blend of the national and the international, the particular and the universal, was nothing less than the image of the Trinity. Somewhat provocatively, Noel even went as far as defending the positioning of flags against the chancel arch of his church by using the doctrine of the Trinity. When his bishop was less than accepting of the ecclesiastical use of the red flag (together with the flag of Sinn Fein and the St George's Cross), Noel turned to the doctrine of God to defend his actions. The red flag, which he saw as symbolising the universal community (presumably representing God the Father), was balanced with the flag of the particular national community (in this case England and Ireland, representing God the Son and God the Spirit). This was because, he claimed, 'God is fellowship, or, in theological language, Trinity, and [we] believe that from everlasting God was no personal and isolated self-lover, but a community of persons bound together by natural love, justice and mercy in one being'.[2] In what sounds like proto-New Labour rhetoric (which would probably have shocked the far more radical Noel) he claimed that '[v]ariety in unity is the fundamental law for the well-being of individuals, of nations and of mankind'. Adding a Christian gloss, he went on:

> For Christians who have really mastered the meaning of the Faith, this conviction is strengthened by our belief in the source of our life as a Sociality, God the Trinity, the One in Many and the Many in One. We believe that there is both unity and variety in the Social Being from whom the world proceeds and in Whom the world is sustained, and that the secret of that being is better expressed by the variety in unity of the rich chord than by the thin unity of the solitary note.[3]

In the introduction to his rather more sophisticated book, *Jesus the Heretic*, Noel speaks of the 'Blessed Trinity as the Basis of a New World Order'. It is 'the will of the Triune God,' he claims, 'to inspire men to renew the world in such a way as to make it the perfect expression of His own Being'.[4] Against such a trinitarian theology, according to Noel, both the ancient Arians and modern Individualists conceived of God as the great distant dictator in the sky. The Arians, that party of 'court flunkeys and flatterers . . . believed in God as a solitary tyrant in a far-away heaven, too great to come down and sojourn with man' who was 'best represented on earth by a solitary and all-powerful Emperor; whose will none might question'.[5] Noel's *Credo* was expressed in the epilogue to *Jesus the Heretic* in terms of a power of community stemming from a God who was himself community: it was in consequence the task of Christians to re-create a world in which there was an 'interplay of initiative and co-operation'.[6] For Noel, then, there was a direct correlation between the doctrine of God and communitarian political action.

More recently, a broad range of popular and academic writers have been attracted to similar ideas of community and communion in God, and have likewise drawn direct political implications from the doctrine. Kenneth Leech, for instance, who has recently retired as a 'community' theologian, stands in the radical tradition of Noel. He calls one of his collections of essays *The Social God*, and begins with a bold claim that Christianity is 'social because God is social, and it is involved because God is involved. . . . The doctrine of the Trinity is essentially the assertion of the social nature of God.'[7] He goes on to maintain that 'the doctrine of the Trinity is an assertion that within the Godhead itself there is society and equality of relationship and that humanity is called to share in that divine life'.[8]

There is a striking similarity between such a claim, which provides the theological underpinning for Leech's popular discussion of the spirituality of resistance, and the far more sophisticated theological approach of the Brazilian liberation theologian, Leonardo Boff. Writing from a completely different context, he offers a similar diagnosis in his *Trinity and Society*, pointing to the 'mystery of perichoresis [mutual indwelling], of the trinitarian communion and the divine society' as a 'model for any just, egalitarian (while respecting differences), social organization'. The divine community thereby offers a model for participation and equality that 'fires the understanding of the oppressed'.[9] Indeed, it is essential to hold a concept of God as a communion of three persons in order for society to be properly structured:

> society needs to be a conjuncture of relationships of communion and participation. . . . The disintegration of trinitarian understanding is due to our losing the memory of the essential perspective of the triune God: the *communion* between the divine Persons . . . Communion is the first and last word about the mystery of the Trinity. Translating this truth of faith into social terms, we can say: 'the trinity is our true social programme'.[10]

Against the modern evils of individualism and totalitarianism, this communitarian doctrine of the Trinity offers a 'critical attitude to personhood, community, society and the church'.[11]

The vision Boff presents is one of a balanced and harmonious network of relationships where the social and the individual survive in mutual and necessary interconnection. Although couched in some high jargon, Boff's ideas elevate community as the perfect balance between individual and society. All remain different from one another, but never to the extent that they are disconnected.

> The three 'Differents' uphold their difference one from another; by upholding the other and giving themselves totally to the other, they become 'Differents' in communion. In the Trinity there is no domination by one side, but convergence of the Three in mutual acceptance and giving. They are different but none is greater or lesser, before or after. Therefore a society that takes its inspiration from trinitarian communion cannot tolerate class differences based on power (economic, sexual or ideological) that subjects those who are different to those who exercise that power and marginalizes the former from the latter.[12]

Although Boff is clear that it is not the theologian's specific task to devise particular political models which might best approximate to the Trinity, he nevertheless suggests that a participatory democracy in which individual differences are shared in communion, and where everything is held in common except personal difference, provides the most appropriate model for overcoming the oppressive power relationships of the contemporary social order. And this model has direct ecclesiological consequences: the church is called to be a 'lunary mystery' derived from the 'solar mystery' of the Trinity, which might show to others what a good community might look like.[13]

Close parallels can be drawn between Boff's work and the extended analysis of the doctrine of the Trinity given by the popular German theologian Jürgen Moltmann in *The Trinity and the Kingdom of God*. Moltmann claims that his trinitarian theology has its origins in a blend of certain medieval schoolmen[14] with the Cappadocian and post-Cappadocian Fathers of the Eastern Church, particularly the great synthesiser of doctrine, John of Damascus.[15] Like Boff, Moltmann claims that the Trinity is the great way of balancing the universal with the particular: 'the Christian doctrine of the Trinity provides the intellectual means whereby to harmonize personality and sociality in the community of men and women, without sacrificing the one to the other'.[16] Consequently the Trinity serves as a critique of power and oppression which allows individuals to flourish, but only in communion and relationship to those around them: 'So the Trinity corresponds to a community in which people are defined through their relations with one another, not in opposition to one another, in terms of power and possession.'[17]

For Moltmann, the notion of sociality in God becomes a panacea for the distortions of the modern world, offering a theological critique of the post-Enlightenment stress on consumerist uniformity in liberalism, as well as of the socialist and fascist experiments in social levelling. Here he begins to sound remarkably Third Way. He uses the language of community in a two-pronged assault: on the one hand, he uses notions of reciprocity and mutual dependence to attack liberal tendencies towards the absolutism of the individual where 'everyone sees in the other person a competitor in the struggle for power and possession'.[18] On the other hand, he uses the community of the Trinity to overcome what he calls the clerically dominated 'monotheism' of much theology: 'It is only when the doctrine of the Trinity vanquishes the monotheistic notion of the great universal monarch in heaven, and his divine patriarchs in the world, that earthly rulers, dictators and tyrants cease to find any justifying archetypes any more.'[19] In a later essay, Moltmann summarises his understanding of the Trinity as a model of both church and society in rather purple terms:

> Father, Son and Spirit . . . do not exist with each other, but rather empty themselves on to each other and live in each other by virtue of love. . . . When the church is such 'an icon of the Trinity', she can also become a life-principle of human society: a society without privileges – a society without poverty and need – a society of free and equal persons. Then the Trinity will become our 'social programme', the programme of social personalism, or of personal Socialism. We would overcome the possessive individualism of the West as well as the depersonalising collectivism of the East. We would be able to integrate a human 'culture of sharing' symbiotically into the perichoretic texture of nature and to live and become

> blessed together with the fellowship of the entire creation
> in the fellowship of the triune God.[20]

In such a statement the connections between the Trinity, politics, church and society are direct and boldly drawn. And what is more, phrases like 'culture of sharing' have a decidedly New Labour ring.

There are many other theologians who similarly understand the doctrine of the Trinity as an answer to modern tendencies towards individualism and collectivism, yet who ground their theology using different theological and philosophical systems. In a somewhat idiosyncratic book, *Theology of a Classless Society*,[21] Metropolitan Geevarghese Mar Osthathios understands God as the 'model of perfect individuality and sociality'.[22] He develops his argument for a classless society on the basis of the reciprocity of a human nuclear family.[23] Indeed, he suggests in a somewhat expansive doctrine of the Trinity, the 'new humanity God aims at is not a joint family of grandparents and cousins, but a nuclear family of God the Father, the church the mother, Jesus Christ the eldest brother and the whole humanity as direct brothers and sisters'.[24] Although he recognises that the 'ideal of a classless society is not attainable in history', nevertheless it is kept as a 'model and appropriated as closely as possible'.[25] The new humanity modelled in God overcomes the distortions of Communism, which he sees as 'only a passing stage towards a theistic classless society',[26] replacing it with a kind of democratic egalitarianism. This provides the basis for the 'world brotherhood, a sharing of resources, world government, jobs for all' and the means for combating a whole host of other social evils.[27] While such aims might be laudable, the language used shows how easy it is to slide from metaphors about what God might be like into prescriptions for social policy.

Using a more sophisticated philosophical system and without such a blatant idolisation of the nuclear family, the late Colin Gunton was equally vociferous in his defence of a social doctrine of the Trinity. His principal opponents are those he sees as defending forms of monarchianism or monism in God and who lack a sufficiently differentiated doctrine of the Trinity. Distortions of the doctrine of God lead to a whole host of ills, not least the Enlightenment notion of the autonomous individual. Thus he suggests that 'behind the individualistic concept of the person, whose development has had such disastrous effects on modern

Western thought, there lies a correlative concept of God'.[28] Drawing on John Zizioulas's influential book *Being as Communion*,[29] as well as John Macmurray's *Persons in Relation*[30] (which, as we have seen, was also a favourite text of the young Tony Blair), Gunton stresses over and again that God has 'no true being, apart from communion'.[31] Being and relation, he suggests, although they can be separated in thought, can in no way be separated 'ontologically' (i.e. in their inmost being): to be is to be in relation, otherwise it is simply not real being. From such a conception of God as pure being-in-relation flow both the doctrine of the church and the doctrine of human beings: 'The church is therefore called to be a being of persons-in-relation which receives its character as communion by virtue of its relation to God, and so is enabled to reflect something of that being in the world.'[32]

Similarly, in his broad historical overview of the Western philosophical and theological tradition, *The One, The Three and the Many*, Gunton sees the notion of relationality grounded in the doctrine of the Trinity. This he considers to be the Christian solution to the problem of universals and particulars, or, as he puts it, the one and the many: 'Parmenides and Heraclitus have called the tune and so have obliterated the trinitarian categories which enable us to think of the world – and therefore also culture and society – as both one and many, unified and diverse, particular and in relation.'[33]

Gunton goes on to ask whether there is to be found a vision of things which 'unifies without producing totalitarianism or homogeneity'.[34] The answer to the distorted ontology of the past (which isolates individuals from their wider context), he claims, is the true form of being which requires relationality. Crucially he sees this way of being as rooted in the doctrine of the Trinity. He thus boldly proclaims: since God and human beings are both personal beings, and since personal beings are by their very nature characterised by their relationality, 'of both God and man it must be said that they have their being in their personal relatedness: their free relation-in-otherness'.[35] Sociality or community is thus fundamental to all human beings, and consequently, a 'theology of sociality teaches that those whose being is constituted by the relations to the triune God should succumb to the ideology of neither the one nor the many'.[36] Thomas D. Parker summarises the importance of the social doctrine of the Trinity clearly. He considers that

> the form of life consistent with the trinitarian apprehension of God is a universal community marked by justice and friendship . . . the political meaning of the doctrine of the Trinity comes as an invitation to share in the struggle for that form of human community which expresses the truth symbolised in Christian faith in God the blessed Trinity . . . The One whose unity is a living out of difference, and whose being is in communion with creatures is no sanction for oppression, violation, injustice or tyranny.[37]

God, the perfect being-in-relation, is thus the starting point for all human communities.

Conflict against community

In these various discussions of the implications of the doctrine of the Trinity for life together in society, there is an implicit assumption that the picture of the relationships between the Father, Son and Holy Spirit is able to function as something of a blueprint for human society. God is spoken of in terms of an idealised society which in turn is capable of being mirrored here on earth through the witness of the church. Although this is undoubtedly appealing, it is precisely at this point that problems begin to emerge. All the conceptions of the social doctrine of the Trinity discussed above see God as a community of mutually interdependent persons who necessarily exist in relation. While this may be the case, it does not follow that the sociality of human societies, even ideal ones, is necessarily rooted in such a notion of perfect being-in-relationship. One point is often overlooked: human communities, especially churches, might aim to reflect something of the divine life, but they all share one thing, however perfect they may seem. They always fall short of the divine life.

Factually, it is patently true that human beings do not always act together in conformity of will and action; and yet the claim of the theologians discussed in this chapter is that the social doctrine of the Trinity should provide a vision, as well as a practical model, for humans in society. It is this step in the argument that does not seem to me to be self-evident. It is at the very least questionable that human beings can ever express themselves most fully and perfectly in terms of the harmony and balance of the mutual reciprocity of the divine life. A perfectly constituted divine community might not be the best place to start a political theology, since, at least in the present age, no community can ever be completely marked by the sort of harmony that characterises God. All human communities fall short of perfection: while they might emulate the total reciprocity present in the Trinity they will always at the same time be characterised by the all too human clamours for power, violence and status which distort all communities, including churches.

Inevitably, it would seem, human societies will be marked by conflict rather than harmony. That being the case, theologians and political theorists may need to rethink the foundations of their thought: they will have to show how that conflict itself might be used to build up rather than destroy human communities. The understanding of God as perfect harmony, which characterises so much of the social trinitarianism discussed in this chapter, perhaps expresses a longing for concord and a conflict-free zone, but it seems quite divorced from the creative and constructive conflict that can plausibly be shown to be the foundation for democratic human societies. It does not easily embrace a theology of pluralism and conflict. In this the social doctrine shares much with the language of the common good, which will be discussed in the next chapter.

It may well be that far from being an aberration or even a sinful distortion, the normal and proper condition of society, and even of the church, is one of dispute and conflict, or to put it in more neutral terms, one of a plurality of views and opinions. There will be different solutions to problems, different ways of organising institutions, and different opinions on all sorts of matters, all of which might be clear, coherent and plausible. In many cases there will be very little certainty about how to achieve some sort of consensus: human beings will often not know what it is best to do in a particular situation. The language of a harmonious community, which is a bit like the Trinity, may well be little more than wishful thinking. Instead, it will be important to work with the communities that we have. Most of them do not resemble the divine life at all – and that includes many churches. This means that we will need to address the problem of conflict.

An example from the history of the church serves as a useful illustration. A glance at the fourth and fifth centuries reveals that conflict is the very foundation for orthodoxy: conciliar decisions prove so often to be little more than the temporary resolution, or even the permanent enshrining, of a conflict in doctrine. The decisions made at the Council of Chalcedon in 451, as well as at Nicea and Constantinople in the previous century, may well be 'regulative', as George Lindbeck suggests,[38] but what they regulate is not straightforwardly conflict free. Orthodox Christianity certainly does not remove conflict: indeed, neither peace at any price, nor harmony, strike me as the most obvious characteristic of the doctrinal development of what became orthodoxy. Bitter and sometimes bloody conflict continued long after decisions were made. And that is perhaps because harmony and order are not obviously central to Jesus' proclamation. Struggle with the implications of what it meant to live in the world and in relationship with Christ, with God made flesh, led to division and disunity from the very beginnings of the church.

It seems quite reasonable to suggest that disunity and conflict between competing groups held together in an often fragile communion are the best ways in which we might begin to understand the early church. Put simply, had there been no conflict there would have been no orthodoxy. And similarly, it seems quite plausible to claim that such a state has become the normal condition of the church ever since. As Rowan Williams writes, in entering the church we

> are not spared the cost of conflict or promised a final theological resolution; rather we are assured of the possibility of 're-producing' the meaning that is Christ crucified and risen, through our commitment to an unavoidably divided church – not by the effort to reconcile at all costs, but by carrying the burdens of conflict in the face of that unifying judgement bodied forth in preaching and sacrament.[39]

And the same might be said of political communities: had there been no conflict with rulers and governments there would have been no change in relationships at a political and social level.

It may indeed be the case that such a 'unifying judgement' of God forces all human societies, including the church, into necessary conflict, rather than leading inevitably to harmony and resolution. Consequently, the test of any 'social' doctrine of the Trinity, it seems to me, rests in its ability to handle this conflict which underpins human communities, including churches. The doctrine of the

Trinity may well help in bringing some conflicts to a temporary solution, but it will also give rise to new tensions and conflicts. The principal problem which emerges from the authors discussed above, however, is that all we have to go on is God's *perfection*. Such perfection seems so utterly different from real human societies that there is little space left for the notion of conflict, healing and restoration. Yet these are the very structuring characteristics of a dynamic human and political society. For the exponents of the social doctrine of the Trinity, it is as if by somehow sharing in the life of God we would be removed from the conflicts at the heart of human life.

To use the example of one of the theologians discussed earlier in this chapter, one might ask whether what Moltmann has really achieved is little more than the portrait of something resembling a green, social market, federal republic in heaven which we need to replicate on earth. However, the notion of a God relating with himself and us in perfect perichoretic union is rather distant from even the most sophisticated and decentralised form of democratic polity. As the German experience reveals, there will often be conflicts between the centre and the periphery. Instead of harmony and shared perceptions of right and wrong and of what counts as the common good, there will frequently be little more than rough and ready solutions to political problems enacted through temporary coalitions and compromises. It does not seem to me to be very helpful to bring the doctrine of the Trinity to this thinking at all. Instead, knowing that we have to make decisions in the full knowledge that we might be misguided and not know whether what we are doing is right, and even that our opponents might equally be right, ought perhaps to make us a little more humble and ready to embrace pluralism with open arms. It seems the logical consequence of living in a human rather than in a divine society.

In a recent book, *Participating in God*, Paul Fiddes has emphasised the overcoming of the tension between individuality and community in the model of trinitarian relationships, which are not self-contained but are relationships into which we are drawn. Language about the trinitarian God, that 'event of relationships', is the language not of the passive observer but the active participant. This is a theology of absorption where 'perichoresis' becomes the key concept. It is explained in terms of dancing – a wordplay invited by the Greek. Yet this is not a dancing merely between a threesome: rather there is an invitation which flows out to human beings to join in the same dance. Whether such a dance can include the conflicts at the heart of human life is altogether another question. After all, dances can be ritualised warfare embodying human conflict in symbolic form. If God is to continue to relate to the world then the tensions and conflicts of real concrete human relationships have to participate in the dance. What was beautiful might soon begin to look very ugly; but it is precisely in that ugliness that we have to do theology.[40]

As will be shown in more detail in the next two chapters, however, further problems emerge when the pluralist situation is overlooked. Indeed, to assume the normativity of certain human communities (and if a community is divine it will be absolutely normative) can serve to limit pluralism altogether. As James Mackey writes in a particularly trenchant criticism of Moltmann: 'the projection onto an immanent divine society of structures of social relationships destined thereafter for re-entry into our human task of building a better world can carry . . . an absolute normativeness and a foreclosure on other options, which are the hallmarks of ideology everywhere'.[41] Similarly, in a provocative article written shortly before his death, David Nicholls, one of the most important theological exponents of political pluralism, also points to the ideological implications of Moltmann's theology: 'A highly integrated and conflict free image of the Trinity will lend support to the kind of social organisation which will leave little room for freedom in the modern world.'[42] And in response to such questions one might suggest that a different social understanding of the Trinity might even make space for conflict in God himself: there is after all nothing necessarily conflict free about the statement that the all-powerful one who creates the world is one and the same as the man who dies on the cross and who rises for our salvation. And that ought to prevent us from resting content with any straightforward solutions. My suggestion is that harmony and unity may not perhaps be all there is to a good community – indeed there might be a need for opposition, for conflict, in order to grow; and furthermore (and more contentiously), it might even be possible to see conflict, or at the very least, tension at the heart of our picture of God. As Nicholls wrote: 'We are urged to think of God as a "society" – but what kind of society or community? A good society, undoubtedly. But what is a good society like? What degree of unity is appropriate to a human social group?'[43]

There is a sense in which Moltmann, at least in his earlier writings, is aware of this potential for conflict in God. He movingly stresses the tension between the Father and the Son on the cross in *The Crucified God*;[44] and yet the tension is reconciled in the love which, while recognising the reality of contradiction, ultimately overcomes it in something resembling a Hegelian synthesis.[45] Such a resolution, however, might be premature even within the Godhead: instead of the Spirit of 'life, love and election' proceeding from the death of the Son, the 'godforsaken one', there might instead be a Father and a Son who cannot be drawn so readily together. The picture of God in the gospels is not simply one of harmony, but also one in which conflicts can be glimpsed.

While it is true that Jesus proclaims God as the compassionate, loving, merciful Father, this needs to be read alongside that other picture of God as judge, at least if the Gospel of Matthew is to be taken seriously: he will banish the wicked to that place where there is weeping and gnashing of teeth. And if we try to draw together those seemingly incommensurate attributes, it might be possible to develop a different conception of God from that maintained by the exponents of the social doctrine of the Trinity. As Nicholls suggested, again somewhat provocatively:

> There must be, within our conception of God, a place for justice, and that traditionally, among Christians . . . has been symbolised by the Father. But also God is merciful and forgiving. . . . But mercy and justice are in principle opposed to each other and in conflict. The claims can be resolved in the concrete case only by an act of practical judgement (*phronesis*). The contradictory nature of the two principles makes it difficult to incorporate them into a monolithic monotheism. If, however, the Son embodies the principle of mercy, we can make sense of the passages in the New Testament where he is seen as interceding for us to the Father. . . . What sense can these images make unless they assume that there is within the life of the Godhead a conflict between the Father and the Son, a conflict of interests whose resolution is only possible in the concrete case? The Son, in interceding as

our advocate, indeed appeals to, and assumes, an inherent
mercy and disposition to forgive in the Father, which is
manifested in the Spirit's healing and transforming
action.[46]

This understanding, which may admittedly be somewhat over-
stated and possibly even verge on tritheism, seems to me nevertheless to imply that we resolve the problem of the Trinity not
primarily by embarking on speculations about the being of God,
however attractive these might appear. Instead, to think about the
nature of God requires us to exercise our practical wisdom: how
does this or that particular relationship or situation reflect the
competing and contradictory strands in God, and are they capable
of reconciliation and transformation? How are justice and mercy
to be combined? How is God's all-loving nature to be reconciled
with the moral demand for justice? As Nicholls writes: 'Conflict
can be constructive [and] when we consider the "internal" life of
the Godhead, an acceptance of conflict will help us to take
seriously the radical counter-claims of justice and mercy and to
forestall an image of God in which mercy completely swamps
justice.'[47]

Nicholls uses more moderate language in his magnum opus,
Deity and Domination: 'while I would not wish to replace a "consensus" model of the triune God by a "conflict" model, it may be
well to acknowledge what bishops call a "fruitful tension" in our
inevitably crude attempts to portray relations between the persons
of the divine Trinity'.[48] The answers are not given – knowing what
God is like is rather more akin to the coalition-building of the
political process which involves us in temporary and piecemeal
solutions.

The particular situation is transformed, is drawn into contact
with God, as we do the relating in each particular concrete case in
the exercise of our practical wisdom. Putting the tensive principles
of justice and mercy into practice moves us forward in the transformation of a world founded on injustice and lack of compassion.
And maybe that sense of experimentation in looking at the implications of the God revealed in Jesus Christ thrusts us forward into
a world transformed by the Spirit, which moves into a temporary
settlement of justice and mercy, but which does not reconcile the
conflict too soon in a mutually interdependent yet ultimately

detached community. That at least is a suggestion for the transformation of politics which will be taken up in the final chapter.

Conclusion

It does not seem too far-fetched to suggest that the importance of the doctrine of God for politics is the very tension between the different attributes of God. Trying to work out how to live life in the image of God is not something that is *fixed* in its formulation, but rather it points towards the constant need for practical transformation, for resolving the conflict for the time being. Doctrinal solutions, like the compromises of politics, are temporary and very partial settlements which are always open to change and development. This political model lies at the heart of human conversation; and it rests too at the heart of each practical act of theological wisdom. Understanding the implications of Christian doctrine is akin to making political decisions. It will not be something fixed and final, but will instead be ongoing and provisional. It will be based on a dialogue between different players that does not paper over the cracks but which recognises the differences and divisions which inevitably result from human uncertainty.

So what I am suggesting is that doctrine is something that only becomes meaningful in its contact with the practical and provisional solutions we make in our lives together as Christians: God's being is manifested in the practical activity of solving the problems of life together. Christianity is thus a life, not a set of propositions, and cannot be based simply on an ontology, even an ontology of being-in-relationship, however appealing: instead it is founded on a God who was alive as we are alive, and who is present with us in today's world. That will mean that we can never rest content with what may ultimately prove to be facile solutions – and we are thereby forced to engage again in the messy conflict-ridden thing we call human relationships (just as God did in Christ). And if doctrine is about giving voice to this God, then it will be equally messy: all we can achieve are compromises, temporary solutions and provisional statements, but never consensus or harmony. Harmony may be a vision and an inspiration, but it hardly characterises the reality of human relationships.

In facing life, Christians, like all other human beings, should not be afraid of conflict. It is through conflict, or at least 'creative tension', that solutions – albeit provisional and piecemeal – begin to emerge. Alternatives achieve little, except perhaps the bureau-cratisation of conflict in the paternalism of church or state. And these do little more than bolster a status quo where change becomes impossible in a settlement that cannot be questioned: the clergy, like the bureaucrats or the managers, know best. In both church and state such a political theory, which often masquerades as something benevolent and progressive (as with Third Way politics), can have sinister implications: a harmonious God (like a harmonious community) is of little assistance to those who are oppressed by systems of exploitation and international trade. In short, if God is to have something to do with the struggles at the heart of human life, this means that a solution to the problem of the Trinity only begins to emerge in the art of living: and that requires a practical, piecemeal and humble wisdom which offers no simple answers, and often no answers at all. In this it is no different from politics, as the next chapters demonstrate.

CHAPTER 5

Communities and Pluralism

The problem of exclusion

This chapter takes up themes begun earlier in the book, discussing again the concept of community, particularly as it relates to the cognate idea of the common good. It would of course be rash for any Christian to deny the importance of community. One does not have to be a John Donne to realise that no man is an island, that none of us is an isolated individual; at the most fundamental level we all require some sort of community and joint effort to satisfy our basic human needs. To take a trite example: having completely failed to grow a single bean in my extensive garden I am aware that without other people I would eventually fade away. Growing crops in England may not be quite the communal effort it was two hundred years ago, but some sort of community is still necessary for the provision of food. It may be more global, but still a network of interactions is vital to sustain the world's population – including incompetent or unlucky vegetable gardeners like me. But the sort of community presupposed by the rhetoric of the Third Way politicians as well as their theological counterparts discussed in the previous chapter goes beyond this basic understanding. For many politicians community language is soon invested with vague notions of belonging to something bigger, of submerging one's individuality into a group with which one wholly identifies and which becomes the backbone for the organisation of society. It is all too easy for the rhetoric to magnify the corporate at the expense of the individual. And for many Christians, as I showed in the last chapter, this kind of belonging is demonstrated most clearly in God, who is himself a kind of perfect, mutually interpenetrating community. To some he is a perpetual if rather incestuous dance.

Such language, however, can easily get carried away. Belonging to a community, even one that seeks to model itself on the divine community, might be all well and good for people who are able to get along and who share a common set of objectives and values. But it does not help much when people disagree, when there are conflicts between individuals and groups: as I suggested in the last chapter, conflict, or at least serious and often disruptive tension, characterises all human societies (and that includes churches) and needs to be addressed at a fundamental level by all those who would seek to organise societies. The crucial questions that need to be asked, it seems to me, are these: given the situation of conflict, then what sort of community do we need and who is a member of that community? How far does belonging to one community set one against another community? How far does community language serve to mask conflict and to impose a restrictive homogeneity?

It is my contention that a realistic politics will be able to handle conflict constructively, creating a sense of pluralist dialogue which does not seek to impose uniformity but which recognises difference between communities coexisting within the limited state. This chapter begins the discussion of pluralism by exposing some of the ways in which community language stifles such pluralism and denies constructive conflict. I will once again be taking a deliberately sceptical stand that is suspicious of community language as applied to politics and ethics. I will continue the critique begun in the last chapter by looking in more detail at the problems associated with the political elevation of communities and more particularly the popular, but to my mind often dangerous, language of the 'common good'. This concept can all too easily serve to suppress pluralism and dialogue, the most important aspects of a well-functioning democracy.

Communities and identity: some twentieth-century examples

The principal reason for my scepticism is straightforward: a quick glance at twentieth-century history reveals that communities have often functioned best in terms of shared values and identity when they have defined themselves against other communities, when they have been deliberately anti-pluralist. Community is as much the problem as the solution. To take just one historical comparison: in Europe before the first world war, many social commentators, from the sociologists Max Weber and Émile Durkheim to the English social commentator Charles Masterman, detected social fragmentation and dislocation from the traditional structures of society (what Durkheim called 'anomie'). Indeed, there was a remarkable degree of unanimity between these thinkers about the social effects of the painful transition to modernity: as people were uprooted from their villages and traditional forms of life so there was a breakdown of the old communal ties, as well as increasing levels of alienation and bureaucratisation. For very many people pre-first world war European society was marked by an all-pervasive social crisis.[1] Not surprisingly, many leaders in the church and in politics sought for a greater sense of integration in society and for a return to the 'traditional values' of something called community.

It comes as no surprise to learn that for many people from across the social and political spectrum the outbreak of the first world war was greeted almost as an answer to their prayers.[2] It was, in Roland Stromberg's striking phrase, the 'antidote to anomie'.[3] The war offered a renewed sense of belonging and identity which appeared to have broken down in the fragmented society that accompanied mass industrialisation. In 1914 people found it easy to unite behind the nation state in the time of national crisis: what was true in Britain was equally true in Germany and France. In Germany, the so-called 'Ideas of 1914' with their values of communal identity and national unity dominated the rhetoric of the period. Similar sentiments of national belonging were expressed across the continent.

It is not difficult to find other twentieth-century examples. In the Cold War climate of the 1950s and 60s, it was easy for nations from both West and East to unite against a perceived or actual enemy. The outsider, either communist or capitalist, was seen as an ever-present threat. It does not take a huge feat of the imagination to see something similar at work in the contemporary world following the collapse of Communism after 1989: for most of the remainder of the twentieth century, new or nascent nation states have sought strength in communal identification against a per-ceived or actual enemy. What was true in the inter-war years is equally true today. In the fragmentation that has followed the breakdown of the Soviet Union and Yugoslavia, the values of ethnic and national communities have become inextricably inter-twined, and ancient animosities have resurfaced. Through all this it would be difficult to deny that the Serbs and Chechens, as well as many other nationalities of the Balkan states and of the former

Soviet Union, have discovered a new sense of communal identity.[4] But it is an identity often bought at the expense of pluralism.

At a global level nations have continued to identify themselves against perceived or actual foes. Following the atrocities of 11 September 2001 the so-called war against terror has become a means of redefining foreign policy against a less easily identifiable foe. Similarly the rhetoric of the 'axis of evil' in President Bush's State of the Union speech of 2002, and the resulting war to bring about regime change in Iraq, was based on the projection of evil on to a group of three more or less developed states on the other side of the globe. Whatever one might conclude about the plausibility of the threats posed by such regimes through the state sponsoring of terrorism, what is important for my argument is the strength of the rhetoric which separates one community from another. Those countries who do not toe the line are derided as 'rogue states' and are condemned to life outside the political process. The goal of international policy is to bring such states back into the process – if necessary by force. They can even become 'terrorist states' which pose the same threat as terrorists and which need to be dealt with using the same emergency powers. As Tony Blair put it in a speech in January 2003: 'States which are failed, which repress their people brutally, in which notions of democracy and the rule of law are alien, share the same absence of rational boundaries to their actions as the terrorist.'[5]

The rhetorical importance of warfare in achieving communal identity might help explain why, as I showed in Chapter 2, Tony Blair has always spoken in Churchillian tones: there is no time like the present for making the decision to fight the war against poverty, exclusion, crime or indeed Saddam Hussein.[6] And that rhetorical use of the language of warfare should alert us to the fact that communities can be destructive as well as constructive. My fear is that much contemporary political rhetoric, as well as the accompanying theology, has been far too ready to adopt the idea of community without paying sufficient attention to this shadow side. Communities, like the social integration they represent, are morally ambiguous: they can be forces for both good and evil.

How common is the 'common good'?

Sometimes the values of 'community' have been enshrined in notions of the 'common good'. Indeed, this term has been used by theologians of many denominations as well as by politicians, apparently with very little questioning. The term even made its way into Anglican liturgical language in the Church of England's short-lived *Alternative Service Book* of 1980 and has survived in *Common Worship*.[7] It can be found in some modern hymns, as, for instance, 'God of freedom' by Shirley Murray, which contains strong sentiments ending with the common good. The second verse reads:

> Rid the earth of terror's torture,
> You whose hands were nailed to wood:
> hear the cries of pain and protest,
> you who shed the tears and blood:
> move us in the pow'r of pity,
> restless for the common good.[8]

While such sentiments and a clamour for justice might be laudable, it still begs the question as to who precisely decides on the content of the common good. Is the good common for those who do not share such a faith in the God of freedom? The concept of the common good seems to me to be as slippery as that of community.

The 'common good' sounds very similar to Tony Blair's 'overarching concept of the public interest' which was discussed in Chapter 2, and can all too easily become a euphemism for the particular values of the powerful or political or social elites. Used slightly differently it can easily become the exclusive preserve of the defenders of traditional values. In this way 'common good' language can become the method by which a small group seeks to harness power for its own ends or to control the public discourse. The question of who defines the 'common good' and whose interest it serves needs to be asked again and again.[9]

The tendency towards defining the common good on behalf of others can be easily perceived in some of Tony Blair's remarks from the late 1990s onwards. In September 1999, for instance, he could claim: 'We need to find a new national moral purpose for this new generation. People want to live in a society that is without prejudice, but is with rules, with a sense of order.' And in this creation of a 'new national moral purpose', he went on, government, which he sees as providing something of the conscience of the nation, can 'play its part'.[10] What is left for the many different groups who make up modern British society but who do not wish to identify with a national moral purpose to contribute to the moral debate is left open; how far the rights of those many minority groups who might disagree with his vision are to be protected is conspicuously not addressed.

From a quite different perspective, the so-called Moral Majority in the United States and its many kindred groups like the Coalition for American Values offer other good examples: their definitions of what counts as good might be common to their members, and it might even be the case that they constitute a majority in some parts of the society, but the extent to which the common good is common to everybody is altogether another question. To put it rather clumsily: a self-proclaimed definer of the common good can easily exclude those who do not share in a particular good's commonality. The obvious problem of common good language is this: where a majority defines the common good, the minority can easily lose its voice. A further problem is created when the institutions of the state are used to enforce the common good, which can simply become a means by which a dominant group seeks to further its own particular ends often at the expense of other groups. Enforcing a national moral purpose, a common good, or some other imposed project clamouring for national moral uniformity can rapidly become the cipher for something anti-pluralist which may easily become oppressive to minorities.[11] Tabloid definitions of the common good can be remarkably effective instruments for attacking the lifestyles of those who might not be so ready to share their understanding of the common good.

A case study: 'Moral Regeneration' in South Africa

In this context the example of post-Apartheid South Africa offers some interesting recent lessons about the political use of common good language. The outsider visiting South Africa is immediately struck by the extraordinary levels of security, where even relatively modest properties are protected by razor wire, ferocious dogs, and signs warning of armed response units. Although there is some debate over the actual (as against perceived) levels of crime, it is clear from bald figures like the murder rate that the society is, at least in some places, extremely violent. Other statistics, including the rate of HIV/AIDS infection, which affects up to one quarter of the total South African population, as well as the high numbers of reported rapes and incidents of domestic violence, also seem to indicate the breakdown of traditional family and kinship ties. Such ties have historically formed the backbone of the different communities in South Africa, even during the worst years of Apartheid. In addition, there are other signs of social alienation, including high levels of gambling (which the present administration appears to be doing little to discourage), as well as widespread alcohol and drug abuse.

The principal underlying cause of these social problems is undoubtedly the existence of massive income differentials between the various population groups: in 1994 black Africans comprised 75.3 per cent of the population of South Africa but earned a mere 39 per cent of the national income.[12] Alongside this are the demographic effects of the segregation policies of the Apartheid era whereby families were split up and whole groups forcibly deported. The legacy of Apartheid will last for a very long time yet. Given these problems, it comes as little surprise that many politicians, who have to court popularity and who always have half an eye on re-election, have sought shorter-term remedies for the apparent breakdown of morality. These seem far easier than widespread income redistribution or population movement. Improving moral behaviour or 'moral regeneration' among citizens has become a government priority.

President Thabo Mbeki could thus speak of the central importance of 'Moral Regeneration' in his State of the Nation address on 8 February 2002.[13] The language of moral regeneration was to be used as a means of

> inculcating in us and our youth that service to the people, selfless commitment to the common good, is more valuable than selfish pursuit of material rewards. Productive investment is more valuable than aimless gambling in markets for derivatives. Payment for honest work is more fulfilling and sustainable than theft. Children and women are there to be respected, not to become targets of abuse.

While such sentiments might be uncontroversial in themselves, two related questions nonetheless emerge from the notion of the 'common good' which the President used in this statement: first, what precisely is the common good in this context, and who defines it and the forms of moral regeneration that will bring it about? Second, and perhaps more crucially, do all South Africans from the large number of different groups, many of which were until very recently extremely hostile to one another, share many, or even any, core or common values? It seems to me to be incumbent on politicians who are prepared to use the language of the common good to identify precisely what they mean when they use the language.

In the South African context this is especially pressing, given the complex history of population movement, current demographic inequalities and, in recent times, the sometimes outright hostility between different groups. It might even be the case that to look for a common good in the present situation of South Africa is to look for far too much. And furthermore, it might lead those concerned to avoid serious discussion of the more concrete economic and demographic issues that need to be addressed before a common South African identity can be formed. The creation of such an identity needs to be balanced, it seems to me, by the competing values of pluralism, as well as tolerance of those with very different understandings of this identity. There may be the need for a common good, but it is likely that its content will have to be reduced to a minimum rather than maximised if diversity and pluralism are to be protected. A common good is required only to the extent that it allows the diverse communities that compose society to flourish rather than to destroy one another.[14]

However, this limited notion of the common good has not been dominant. Third Way politics has expressed itself in South Africa in terms of the Moral Regeneration Movement (MRM) with its resonances of Frank Buchman's Moral Rearmament Movement of the 1940s and 50s. In the preparations for the launch of the movement a few months after Thabo Mbeki's State of the Nation address, Jacob Zuma, Deputy President, spoke of the MRM in terms similar to those of Mbeki. He saw the project as that of reviving the nation's morality through re-establishing close-knit kindred feeling; in his speech he made much use of the African terms 'ubuntu' or 'botho', interpreting them in a decidedly communitarian fashion:

> Our people have high moral values which are evident in all our cultures. We must transform the anti-social acts that threaten our country. The MRM recognises and endorses this concern, and is a framework to encourage, facilitate, sensitise and network the response in every sector of our

society. It envisages a confident community with a strong moral fibre. Its mission is to revive the spirit of ubuntu/botho, using all the resources available in government and civil society. It is committed to establishing the values expressed in our Constitution.

In his closing speech at the summit which launched the MRM at Waterkloof Airbase on 16 April 2002, Zuma was even more explicit in calling for a common South African identity. He spoke of the need for a common commitment to 'the denunciation of an immoral social order and a promotion of a collective common South African identity as envisaged in the Constitution'. Again, however, the question of how this common identity related to the extraordinarily pluralist society that constitutes contemporary South Africa, composed as it is of a whole range of different communities, did not receive much attention. The need for a common identity with its 'strong moral fibre' still remains unproven. Indeed, it might be better to begin by searching for ways in which different communities can learn to live with one another without a common good but also without aggression and violence, rather than getting them to agree on some sort of shared moral programme – a suggestion which will be developed in the next chapter.

South Africa, perhaps even more than other countries, needs to guard against the use of the institutions of the state to further a particular community's ends and to define the 'common good' in terms of one group's values, however benign this might appear. The problem with common good language is that it tends in this direction simply because of its use of universals: what is common must be true for all people (whether they like it or not). For this reason common good language, like the language of community to which it is closely related, can rapidly become oppressive and anti-pluralist.

The role of the state

In post-Apartheid South Africa the government has sought the aid of intermediate organisations in its task of instilling its understanding of the common good. Many have been ready and willing to side themselves with government policies. However, it is important to ask to what extent the institutions of civil society – including churches – should be responsible for implementing the government's vision of what constitutes the common good. The government has shown a great desire to use the resources of civil society and to build partnerships with non-governmental agencies for the promotion of Moral Regeneration. This is apparent in the submission to the MRM Summit by the lead minister on Moral Regeneration in the Social Sector, Dr Ben Ngubane, Minister of Arts, Culture, Science and Technology. In a very lengthy sentence he claimed:

> For government to achieve the regeneration of morals to the society, the Summit should reflect its intended objectives on strategies and measures to reconstruct the social values of the new democratic South Africa, facilitate the evolution of a dynamic mass movement to help and support the government–civil society initiative in planning an effective programme of action for the moral renewal of our society and design [a] vigorous programme of action for sustainable Moral Regeneration campaign following the Summit to promote the creation of an ethical, caring and corruption-free society.[15]

While obviously nearly all the institutions of civil society, especially the churches, would share the government's ideal of crime reduction and community formation, at the same time there is a problem that emerges from government–civil society partnerships, and which raises fundamental questions about the role of the churches in the state. If the churches become the means for the implementation of government policy, to what extent can they retain a critical distance from the government? If they disagree with the government's ideas of what constitutes the common good, then what space can there be for challenging those in political power? If churches side solely with the majority, then what space is left for them to be protectors of minorities?

This problem is especially pressing in a democracy: if the government can claim legitimacy through having been popularly elected by a majority (which was obviously never true in the Apartheid years), then what right does the church (or any other institution of civil society for that matter) have to question its policy? It is interesting to note that in 2001 President Mbeki had met with leaders of five different religions to discuss mutual co-operation in the building up of a non-racial South Africa. The hazard of co-operation, however, is the extent to which 'partner-ship' leads to the silencing of the church's critical voice. For churches which previously gained their identity through opposi-tion to the state, including the Church of the Province of Southern Africa which, under the charismatic leadership of Archbishop Desmond Tutu, was such an important member of the anti-Apartheid coalition, this can easily lead to a crisis of identity in the present.[16]

Conclusion

Before going on to discuss the role of churches and other agencies of community formation in the next chapter, I will conclude this chapter by summarising what I see as the main problems emerging from community and common good language. First, it is important to stress the almost universal use of community language by both left and right in addressing the problems of the loss of social cohe-sion that comes about through large-scale industrialisation (and in recent years, de-industrialisation). Second, as the South African example clearly demonstrates, the state can easily see itself as the agency of community and bearer of tradition, thereby becoming the enforcer of moral consensus. Third, as the revival of ethnic and religious nationalism shows, exclusive communities often identified with nations can easily see themselves as all-powerful communities to which all other communities are subservient.[17] Such pretensions can be appealing but are frequently either ludicrous or downright dangerous. Finally, common good language and the language of community can easily elide into one another in popular political discourse. Governments define something called a common good which communities exist primarily to foster and to uphold. Yet, as I have suggested, communities themselves might not be very interested in the notion of a common good at all and may not even see it as desirable. The fundamental inconsistency in the two forms of language frequently appears to go unnoticed. Communities often work against the common good.

So much recent political and theological language is working – consciously or unconsciously – with the concept of a strong and universal moral community which provides the backbone of society. In many ways this does not seem too far removed from William Temple's wartime collectivist vision. Despite the rhetoric of modernisation or 'community', the paternalist and collectivist past has quietly returned. Calls for 'community' and the 'common good' do not seem to be able to protect the pluralist structure of contemporary Britain. Blair and New Labour might be relatively benign, but the danger of government coercion is always present: state-imposed community is potentially always a threat. Consequently, it is important to ask whether there might be alternatives to the Third Way language of community and moral consensus. Is there a viable alternative which respects diversity, pluralism and constructive conflict but which still allows for individuals to flourish in participatory communities? What will be developed in the remainder of this book is a form of participative democracy which guarantees pluralism without the need for a strong centralised state. This is a vision which allows very different people to participate in a single society without any recourse to problematic concepts like the 'common good'.

CHAPTER 6

Communities, Civil Society and the Reconstruction of Politics

Through the course of this book it has become clear that some form of revitalised community has been regarded as an almost universal panacea to a whole panoply of problems of the modern world. What is conspicuously lacking in most language, however, is any expression of precisely what sort of thing a community might be, as well as how it relates to other communities and to the structures of civil society and the state. Answers to such questions are crucial in the reorientation of politics towards democratic pluralism. For New Labour and for Third Way politics in general the politics of community is regarded as the basis of all moral consensus and is required for its whole political programme. Despite this there is virtually nothing in the rhetoric that reveals precisely where and how 'community' is to be expressed. Few politicians have managed to speak except in extraordinarily vague terms. All that can be gleaned is that communities confer some sense of belonging and identity on their members. In this way, the community simply becomes something (anything?) that fills, as Jonathan Sacks put it, a 'certain emptiness at the heart of common life'.[1] That being the case, one might ask whether a community is vague enough to be identified with a whole range of institutions and groups. These might be a village, a church, or a social club. But it is difficult to know where to draw the boundaries: do regular members of a bingo hall or a gym constitute a community? All I think that can be said for the moment is that people who belong to communities identify with the values of that group and to some extent at least are prepared to be obedient to the rules of the community. Communities are in some sense what Gerhard Lohfink (in discussing the early church) termed 'contrast-societies'.[2] This implies some form of submission on the part of the individual, which will usually be voluntary. In this sense a community will be different from a state, even though states will often use the language of community. As many commentators have noted, community formation belongs to the sphere in between the state and the individual.

This intermediate sphere is often dubbed 'civil society', briefly defined as that 'intermediate associational realm between state and family'.[3] Such an understanding patently moves away from the Marxist understanding in terms of the moral and economic agencies established to legitimise the bourgeoisie, towards a public space that contains voluntary organisations and interest groups which act as agents of community-formation. In both neo-liberal and Third Way polities such groups become the principal means for ensuring social participation and the re-creation of the elusive community. In this way the voluntary or 'third' sector is the place where what the communitarian guru, Etzioni, calls the 'spirit of community' might be created.[4] It is in such a voluntary sector that he sees people as bound together by a sense of trust (which many have seen as declining in recent years, particularly since the second world war).[5] The intermediate sphere thus becomes the crucial factor in social formation. Many thinkers have consequently applied community language to the voluntary sector, particularly to participatory bodies like churches and charities.

One of the important theorists of the public sphere, Jürgen Habermas, spoke of civil society as a means of creating social solidarity, defined as the 'ability of individuals to respond to and identify with one another on the basis of mutuality and reciprocity without calculating individual advantages and above all without compulsion. Solidarity involves a willingness to share the fate of the other, not as the exemplar of a category to which the self belongs but as a unique and different person.'[6] Similarly, following the publication of Alasdair MacIntyre's highly influential *After Virtue*,[7] much discussion has also focused on creating communities in civil society, as exemplified by Jonathan Sacks' 1992 Reith Lectures[8] and Robin Gill's *Moral Communities*.[9]

This may be all well and good in theory, but in practice there has been surprisingly little discussion of how such voluntary communities are supposed to relate to governments and states. So often, it seems, civil society is quite distinct from the realm of politics. Its institutions, the primary agencies of community-formation, are incomparably weaker than the state. At present the intermediate sector is so emasculated that it merely offers a further symptom of the restriction and marginalisation of political language: just as the political has been removed from the economic through the triumph of the expert and the auditor, so the sphere of 'community' has been restricted to what has been termed 'civil society' and is consequently depoliticised.

The power of voluntary communities, even where they have attained a statutory function, is seriously weakened when there is little chance of their influencing government policy. Instead, they can easily become little more than secondary agencies in dispensing government initiatives and largesse. They frequently resemble government agencies in their professionalised ethics and often lack a widespread voluntary membership. Many intermediate agencies simply do not see themselves principally as primary organs of socialisation or community-formation and do not require a high degree of commitment on the part of their membership. The bureaucratisation of intermediate organisations is well exemplified by changes to political parties. In the past they often functioned as something like faith-based organisations requiring a very high degree of commitment. Yet this is usually no longer the case: grassroots political parties have declined in membership even faster than other voluntary organisations, and, at least in the Labour Party, voting no longer requires participation or face-to-face contact with other Labour Party members. Being a member of the Labour Party requires no more commitment than belonging to the National Trust.

What emerges from this situation is something deeply disturbing. According to the theorists, the intermediate sector of civil society is absolutely vital for community-formation. Such communities are in turn required to solve the social problems of the wider society. Intermediate voluntary communities are frequently called on to shape the civil and public sphere. At the same time, however, the intermediate sector (as say with the housing associations or the myriad medical charities) is frequently becoming simply another way of putting government policy into action. Many are tantamount to being quangos, but lack any accountability except from the paymaster (which might well be the government). That being the case, there seems little reason why people should socialise themselves through such intermediate organisations. Participatory organisations are marginalised still further. Indeed, as the South

African example discussed in the previous chapter demonstrates, they may simply become all too uncritical agents of state ideology.

For most thinkers, it would appear, the institutions, structures and power of the state and its agencies remain relatively unaffected by the actions of communities. Sometimes it seems as if the real purpose of intermediate communities is to make people content with their lot so that governments can get on with their governing. If churches are the primary agencies of such community-formation, as Blair seems occasionally to suggest, then it would seem that Marx was right. Religions, or at least the communities that religions foster, are little more than opiates to ensure a happy and acquiescent population ready to accede to the government's will. Indeed, it may well be true that belonging to voluntary participatory communities with their shared ethic and sense of corporate belonging will be little more than a leisure-time pursuit. One is thereby socialised simply in one's spare time. Golf clubs, gyms, and possibly even churches, political parties and trade unions, become leisure communities separated off from the state. Sometimes they might be highly effective agents of socialisation. But they lack any political clout: instead they are basically left alone to do their own thing and not to get in the way of the state.

The intermediate sphere of communities is thus frequently marginalised in the face of a detached government and a private sector divorced from worker and consumer alike. Communities inevitably remain separate from where the power lies – from the state itself. The irony is clear: revitalised communities are often called upon to influence the civil and public sphere, yet that very sphere itself is frequently completely marginalised. However communitarian civil society might become, it nevertheless remains quite separate from where political power and sovereignty lie – from the state itself. Social fragmentation – the lack of any sense of community – is obviously a problem, and yet in most solutions which focus on the reconstruction of community, the institutions and the power of the state remain unaffected. The two apparently conflicting dimensions of New Labour policy – the desire to manage change efficiently through audit and control and the elevation of face-to-face communities into the universal value underpinning all politics – are in practice easily reconciled. Because communities are relegated to the voluntary sector they fall outside the direct control of economics. Indeed, it is almost as if the practice of community is purely a private affair. Good moral citizens who organise themselves into communities of mutual aid might even be more effectively managed, as well as being more effective managers. All this is deeply disturbing for the future of democratic politics.

The reshaping of what constitutes a community raises enormous political questions. Indeed, the separation of communities from the realm of politics invites a solid Marxist critique. It seems pertinent to ask: whose interests are being served in the reorientation of moral communities towards civil society and away from the political sphere? And in relation to the issues raised in Chapter 3, what is the relationship between the state and the moral communities? In what sense, if any, can executive agencies and other quangos be seen as moral communities? To what extent do they embody mutuality and participation? And beyond the public sphere, is there any evidence that New Labour has done much to foster communities in the workplace or in places where political power can be expressed? Consequently, it seems to me, overcoming the fragmentation and apathy of modern Western societies through revitalised communities requires something more far reaching than that offered by New Labour – nothing less than a radical rethinking of the structures of the state and the models of authority and sovereignty with which it works.

Redirecting sovereignty

What seems crucial for the future of politics is that communities gain some form of independent political power. The alternatives rest in being dictated to by a centralised state and purveyor of moral values or being marginalised from politics altogether. Instead, what seems to be necessary is to make the intermediate voluntary communities of civil society the starting point for all politics. This form of politics is nothing new, but it has hardly been in the ascendant through the twentieth century. For such a politics to work there must necessarily be a devolution of power from the centre to the periphery, not by way of reluctant concession, but as the foundation of all authority and sovereignty. For most of the twentieth century this style of political thought, known as political pluralism, with its emphasis on the voluntary group, participation and local responsibility, did not seem to be a viable practical political option. In a world based on large power blocs with centralised planned economies, the idea of weakening the sovereignty of the state and transferring authority to intermediate and local associations seemed out of place. Similarly, in terms of the broader British political tradition, a redirection of power away from the centre seems a long way removed from the strong sense of sovereignty which is at least as old as Henry VIII.

Not surprisingly, ideas which flourished for a brief time in the fragmented society of Edwardian England were superseded by the demands of the military organisation required for the first world war and for the continued political struggles that followed. However, the changes in international politics and in our own society since 1989 make Edwardian political theory all the more important. Indeed, it is interesting to note that even Tony Blair once cited one of the fathers of political pluralism, G. D. H. Cole, but offered no elucidation: 'A socialist society that is to be true to its egalitarian principles of human brotherhood must rest on the widest possible diffusion of power and responsibility, so as to enlist the active participation of as many of its citizens in the tasks of democratic self-government.'[10]

Diffusion of power and responsibility seems light years away from the government by audit and depoliticisation of the public sphere analysed above. And yet the idea of political participation in a free pluralist society is crucial for the future of politics. Overcoming the fragmentation and apathy of modern Western societies, while at the same time making a virtue out of pluralism, requires a radical rethinking of the structures of the state as well as the systems of authority and sovereignty with which it works. The political and theological dimensions of this model, which might best be called 'pluralist democracy', will be developed in the remainder of this book.

Thinking the unthinkable: Frank Field and 'social collectivism'

I begin by discussing the thought of a recent influential Christian politician, Frank Field (b. 1942),[11] MP for Birkenhead since 1979, and briefly charged by New Labour with rethinking social security policy. Probably more than any other Labour politician he has sought to rejuvenate some of the important vehicles of community-building from the past, and has been equally critical of many of the corporatist and centralist solutions of the post-war years. Although his theories are deeply flawed he nevertheless retains a firm sense of self-help and community action against the centralism of the welfare state. Field is in many ways an independent thinker who is undoubtedly outside the socialist mainstream. As will become clear, his work has an originality and idiosyncrasy that was never going to endear him to the leadership of his own party: not surprisingly, he has often been a thorn in the flesh of New Labour and was described by David Willetts as 'many Conservatives' favourite politician'.[12] Although he may have risen to glory in the first year of the new administration, he fell from grace equally rapidly. His claim that 'Thinking the unthinkable was never meant to be a task for government'[13] was soon realised in practice. As I will suggest, however, his theory is highly problematic: its return to 'Victorian values', while containing much that is valuable, fails adequately to safeguard pluralism, substituting instead a uniform and highly aristocratic ethic.

Frank Field, through his long career working to alleviate child poverty and as an MP, has frequently sought to address the problems associated with large-scale centralised forms of state socialism. Writing in *Making Welfare Work* in 1995, he claimed that one of the major faults of the welfare state was its stifling of what he called the 'cardinal principle' of self-interest. Welfare dependency, he suggested, destroyed self-love, Christ's second commandment.[14] At the heart of Field's unthinkable thoughts was the notion that collectivist solutions required 'control and ownership' of welfare provision. The anonymous welfare state, he claimed, particularly the pernicious and almost universal practice of means-testing,[15] had destroyed many of the virtues of hard work, thrift and honesty; consequently it needed to be replaced 'so that individual wishes can simultaneously promote new senses of community. . . . Stakeholder welfare provision ushers in a period of popular or social, as opposed to state, collectivism.'[16]

Resisting New Labour's vague talk of rebuilding community, Field has sought practical solutions which recognise the realities of the situation, and which resort less frequently to the 'common good' ethics detectable in so much New Labour rhetoric. Against Tony Crosland-style welfare egalitarianism with its stress on the strong state, Field emphasises the importance of individual freedom and the principles of self-help. Indeed, according to Field: 'One of Crosland's most important successes was to hijack the Labour Party and convert it into a vehicle which saw socialism as being basically about equality.'[17] Against this social levelling, Field's vision is dominated by a 'love thy neighbour as thyself' ethic writ large where both self and neighbour are equally stressed: equality always needs to be tempered by the rights of the individual. In this, Field sees himself as consciously developing the strand of Christian socialism espoused by R. H. Tawney between the wars, which recognised the importance of original sin:[18]

> We are less than perfect creatures and it is partly because of this most fundamental aspect of each of us that a distinction has continually to be made between where we are now and our destiny, on the one hand, and what might be hoped for now in the bosom of the family and what can operate in the wider public arena, on the other.[19]

In distinction to Richard Titmuss' understanding of welfare with its stress on altruism and its downplaying of sin, Field is keen to move towards a realism which places great weight on self-interest: people will only be altruistic, he claims, when there is a recognition that they will reap some benefit for themselves. Indeed, Field does not consider that 'selfless action is a realistic proposition for public as opposed to private conduct'.[20] It thus had to be in the self-interest of the majority to move towards a stakeholder system of welfare.[21] 'Love (altruism) might be expressed within small groups such as families or within very close friendships. But it was not a motive force on which societies could be safely governed.' Consequently, Field writes, 'Thinking the unthinkable on this front was about placing a Christian understanding of mankind centre stage.'[22]

Field's practical proposals for welfare reform centre on the 'stakeholder' idea, which has since become New Labour orthodoxy: people are to be given an interest in their own destiny which thereby serves to overcome something of the alienating effects of impersonal organisation. Here the emphasis is on finding a substitute for the anonymity of large-scale and bureaucratic welfare provision which alienates the citizen and saps 'individual responsibility and initiative'. Field sees this alienation and dependency culture as the major fault of the implementation of the Beveridge Report.[23] Against such centralist bureaucratic solutions he calls for small-scale participative institutions delivering private or charitable provisions, which are far more intimately related to their members. In a speech given in the early months of the first Blair government, Field remarked:

> There are still over 10 million friendly society members in the UK. These organisations are membership bodies based on the ideas of self help, work, savings and honesty. It is around precisely these principles that the Government wishes to reform welfare – and mutual societies may well have a more significant rôle to play in the future than they have had in the immediate past. . . . In conducting our review we need to break out of the 'welfare equals State' mentality.

In short, he concluded, 'We are pledged to break the destructive mould of welfare in which government's only responsibility is to write the cheque and the recipients' only responsibility is to cash it.'[24]

Similar ideas can be found in Field's Bernard Gilpin lectures on pastoral theology given at Durham.[25] While these lectures are noticeably lacking in any theology, they seek to re-establish the ethical basis for socialism, or what he calls a 'moral framework to buttress a new consensus'.[26] The 'big idea' is again about 'opening up opportunities so that individuals (rather than classes) can develop and use their talents to the full. . . . Labour's ethical tradition, built around the importance that should be attached to each individual member of the community, can provide the moral framework within which a more just market economy can flourish.'[27] Field's proposals for welfare reform are quite consistent with this vision. Indeed, he sees his work as the transfer from the realm of the impossible to that of the possible. In another book he cites a rather purple passage from Barbara Wootton with approval:

> The limits of the possible constantly shift, and those who ignore them are apt to win in the end. Again and again I have had the satisfaction of seeing the laughable idealism of one generation evolve into the accepted commonplace of the next. But it is from the champions of the impossible rather than the slaves of the possible that evolution draws its creative force.[28]

Field clearly sees himself as something of a visionary. And here he is prepared, unlike most of his fellow Labour politicians – including members of the Christian Socialist Movement like Tony Blair – to draw explicitly from the Christian tradition. It is also here that his theory, which at first sight looked so promising, sinks into a strange anti-pluralist traditionalism. In an interesting (or less charitably, a bizarre) little book, *The Politics of Paradise*,[29] which, as far as I know, is the only explicitly theological work written by a high-profile British Labour national politician since the second world war, Field draws lessons from both the Bible and the tradition. The Kingdom of God, his central theme, turns out to be both this-worldly and other-worldly, always in the process of completion: 'We know from our own experiences and senses that the Kingdom is not yet established in any full or total sense.'[30] Consequently we have responsibilities to ensure our part in its completion. 'To say that the Kingdom is not built by man does not mean that mankind has no part to play in the kingdom. The reverse is true. The Kingdom – or God's reign – is extended as people, both as individuals and as groups, accept the invitation God offers to become a certain kind of character.'[31] Discipleship is thus about development as a human being, the acquisition of certain character traits which will help bring about God's reign. In describing the Christian character, Field has a liking for Matthew 23:

> Admission to the Kingdom ... is gained by becoming the kind of character who looks, not just to outward actions, but also to inward motives, and who is not merely concerned with resisting the temptations of evil, but with carrying out positive acts. It is achieved by becoming someone who is concerned, not only with personal piety but also with collective sanctity.[32]

This combination of inner and outer, Field claims, should characterise the Christian's approach to politics. In later chapters of the book, which are more visionary and less biblical, he seeks to apply his ideas. Influenced by Lesslie Newbigin's *The Other Side of 1984*, Field attacks the Enlightenment, calling for the return of what Polanyi names the 'fiduciary issue'.[33] While recognising with Newbigin that this cannot result in the impossible dream of a return to Christendom, Field nevertheless urges the 'promotion of a Christian perspective'.[34] In a somewhat strange chapter, he describes the method for this promotion through what he calls, in

Coleridgean terms, 'renewing the clerisy'. He envisages a more educated clergy engaged in moral education primarily through a revitalised system of church schools. In this way the Christian character can be formed in the individual, which in turn will have profound effects on the sanctification of the community.[35] These characters will help convey the 'vision about God's design and the nature of man'.[36] Such a vision Field sees as encapsulated in the 'essence' of Jesus' teaching, the 'duty equally to love God, ourselves and our neighbour. This loving is the agent by which the Kingdom is extended.'[37] The churches, Field holds, should busy themselves with this vision so that by extension it might spread through the whole of society. There is, however, no direct blueprint for trans-ferring vision to reality: Christianity is certainly not the theory of which socialism is the practice (as William Temple once claimed); instead 'the onus is clearly on each one of us to reflect on what [Jesus] has taught, and for each one of us to draw what we think are the relevant conclusions. . . . Only by exercising our free will, and fully trusting in God, can we truly seek the Kingdom.'[38]

Overall, while Field's *Politics of Paradise* lacks a certain coherence, it nevertheless again emphasises the strongly individualist nature of his version of socialism with its stress on loving ourselves at the same time as loving our neighbours. In comparison with much of earlier Christian Socialism, with its strong sense of central planning, as well as the communitarianism of much contemporary Labour thought, Field gives a high priority to freedom. Yet at the same time he moves towards an aristocratic elitism to spread the ideals of the Christian vision, which in a multi-cultural society seems anachronistic to say the very least. A defence of pluralism (and even a recognition of diversity) is noticeably lacking.

The same criticisms hold true for Field as for the defenders of the common good. Who, one might ask, is to define the virtues of the Christian character? And furthermore, do the clergy of a modern church really see themselves (or wish to see themselves) as agents of moral vision through the leaven of the church school? There is something quaintly Victorian about Field's book, as well as his more recent writings which stress the importance of self-help: all this seems distant from the pluralism of contemporary Britain. And it ignores an obvious question: if self-help and the stake-holder concept are at the heart of the provision of welfare, then what becomes of those people who have no stake in anything?

Field's stress on freedom and his return to voluntarism might be an important corrective to the excesses of centralism, but at times his writing can sound somewhat more sinister. He emphasises the *quality* of people's lives and thereby imports a paternalistic ethic which – however desirable it might sound – seems to threaten the centrality of freedom and with it any hope of pluralism.[39] Christianity is transformed into an imposed moralism: the stress on original sin does not seem to be tempered by the sort of humility which might allow for a diversity of opinion. As that most Christian of atheists, Tony Benn, put it in his Tawney Lecture of 1988:

> One . . . priority to which Christian socialists should address themselves is how to unite the ideas associated with fellowship and collective effort with freedom, to make it real in a pluralistic society where equality does not mean uniformity. . . . We have to re-establish the rights of freedom of thought, freedom of speech, the right to be heard and the right to be different. . . .
>
> To be candid, the idea of freedom of this kind has been unwelcome to many who call themselves Christians or socialists . . . and it will always be a struggle to reassert whoever is in power.[40]

The final chapter seeks to meet this challenge by developing a Christian politics which takes pluralism and freedom seriously.

CHAPTER 7

Another Christian Politics: Pluralist Democracy

Through the course of this book I have pointed to some of the problems associated with the calls for community and the depoliticisation of the public sphere. It is, I have suggested, important to preserve individual liberty against the constraints of the group and the state. Nevertheless, there is no guarantee that individual freedom itself is likely to provide a sufficient remedy for the fragmentation of modern society. However problematic they might be, there is still something crucial about participative communities. What seems to be needed is a Christian vision for society which does not necessarily require either notions of the common good, or the formation of the Christian character through some kind of neo-Athenian theory of education, but which regards freedom and its expression in a pluralist society as central to the Christian Gospel. A version of pluralism seems to be the best way to avoid the liberty-denying communitarianism, managerialism and nationalism of New Labour as well as the acquisitive individualism so prevalent in the modern world.

Central to the pluralist vision is an attack on any theory of sovereignty which works from the top down; instead, the state is seen as at best a necessary evil to solve disputes. Against collectivism, which requires strong centralised authority, pluralism works from the bottom up: all power is devolved from the centre. Put bluntly: no authority is needed except where people dispute with one another. In such a system, there is no sovereign parliament, government, party or church dictating the common good, and for that matter no educated elite deciding on what counts as a good character. Nevertheless, if such a society is to function and not collapse into sheer individualism, participation in decisions is required, and some kind of authority is needed: however, instead of being granted a strange quasi-religious status derived ultimately from the divine right of kings, it is simply tied up with the need to resolve conflicts when they might arise. Institutions are thus not alien from those participating in them, but are shaped and reshaped by active engagement. Solving conflicts, or at least learning how to live with them, is at the heart of pluralism.

John Neville Figgis (1866–1919)

Political pluralism flourished briefly in Edwardian England. It was maintained by a group of thinkers who approached the problem of fragmentation and groups from different perspectives. Some names are still fairly well known, as, for instance, G. D. H. Cole and the younger Harold Laski, whose ideas have been recently revived by (among others) the late David Nicholls and Paul Hirst.[1] But one name is central for the development of a Christian political theory which can offer a critique of New Labour-style politics: J. N. Figgis. Figgis was the son of a Brighton minister of the Countess of Huntingdon's Connexion and was educated at St Catharine's College, Cambridge where he came under the influence of the church historian Mandell Creighton, afterwards bishop of Peterborough and London, and of F. W. Maitland, the great legal historian. He gained a brilliant First in 1889, and won a host of prizes. He was received into the Church of England and ordained after a period at Wells Theological College in 1894. After a curacy he became lecturer at his old college from 1896 to 1902.[2] After experiencing a crisis in faith and health, or what would nowadays be called a nervous breakdown, he became Rector of the college living of Marnhull in Dorset from 1902 to 1907.[3]

In 1907 he was received into the Community of the Resurrection at Mirfield in Yorkshire after seeing a play by Bernard Shaw and, as an honorary Fellow of his old college, he alternated in what his biographer called a 'regular pendulum motion between Mirfield fasts and Cambridge feasts'. Freed from parochial and teaching duties he was able to devote himself to writing and preaching, and his publications proceeded steadily from 1907. During his time as scholar–monk he gave the acclaimed Hulsean Lectures in 1908–9[4] and lectured on three occasions in the USA. He was also much in demand as a preacher and retreat conductor, particularly in more fashionable Anglo-Catholic churches.[5] In January 1918 while on his way to the USA, the boat in which he was travelling was torpedoed and shipwrecked off the coast of

Antrim. He never recovered from the trauma of this incident and spent his last days in a mental hospital in Virginia Water, dying on Palm Sunday, 13 April 1919.[6]

Figgis was a great cultural critic of his times, recognising that the complacency of the Victorian period was at an end. In an undated letter written from Marnhull to a Cambridge friend, he commented: 'I do think the clock is running down, the civilisation is revealing its own end times.'[7] Like many other cultural commentators, Figgis recognised fragmentation and loss of meaning. At the very outset of his book *Civilisation at the Cross Roads*, for instance, he announced that 'Something is crumbling all around us. That is clearer every moment.'[8] Later in the same book, he went on in language that sounds decidedly post-modern: 'We live in an age of unparalleled anarchy both moral and intellectual. The confusion of tongues is worse than any Babel of old.'[9] In response, Figgis saw the need to return to a heartfelt faith, but one that did not ignore the gains of the past. In his practical solutions to the crisis of modernity he looked again at history, coming up with some perhaps surprising conclusions.

The revival of political pluralism at the turn of the third millennium might seem somewhat removed from both ecclesiology and the Middle Ages, yet it has Christian roots in the counter-culture of the pre-Reformation Catholic Church. As a historian, Figgis found resources in this tradition. 'Only persons who are ignorant often can describe the Middle Ages as dark.'[10] It has to be said, however, that the political theory of the late Middle Ages, as Figgis claimed in his seminal work on the period, *From Gerson to Grotius*, is an especially dull subject. With a typical irony, he called it a 'literature without charm or brilliancy or overmuch eloquence, voluminous, arid, scholastic, for the most part; dead it seems beyond any language ever spoken. Dust and ashes seem arguments, illustrations, standpoints, and even personalities.'

Although there may well have been more interesting things to study, the political theories of the Middle Ages and the early modern period possessed what he called a 'significant dullness' and were 'worth studying if we would understand the common facts of to-day'.[11] By discovering a political counter-current, which had been all but destroyed by a strange amalgam of pope and prince in the Reformation and post-Reformation struggles (as with Henry VIII), and which had become the source of the excessive claims made for the centralised authority of the state in the modern era, Figgis was able to develop a theological and political model of authority which, he intimates, was more consonant with Christian principles. As I will suggest in my conclusion, this seems to offer a possible basis for a viable alternative to New Labour politics.

Figgis on the authority of the church

In his later work Figgis outlines a practical theory of the church (and by extension a political system) based upon his historical research: thus the principles of federalism, conciliarism and a system of authority quite unlike most modern models of sovereignty (and carried to their extreme by the nineteenth-century papacy) characterise the pluralist ecclesiology developed particularly in *Churches in the Modern State.*[12] This doctrine of the church rested on one simple truth which he saw as exemplified in the history of the post-Reformation church: because there were many different ecclesiastical groups, there could be no monolithic unitary church, since all authority was based on the living authority of those who placed their allegiance in a particular church.

Figgis consequently points to the need for a renewal of 'federalised authority', a form of ecclesiastical sovereignty which he saw as the particular genius of the Church of England. The universal church, in so far as it could be said to exist at all, was a body which depended for its authority on the groups which comprised it, and who conceded to it a specific realm for adjudication in disputes: authority in the church was necessary not in itself but only when it was required to settle disputes. All authority had ultimately to rest with the living parts of the church, the worshipping communities, and any wider authority was parasitic upon this:

> The theory on which the English Church . . . bases its doctrine is the direct opposite [of the ultramontane theory where all authority is gathered at the centre]. The authority of the Church is not an abstract doctrine deduced from the notion of unity; but it is a synthesis of all the living parts of the Church. True, a connection exists between them, or one could not talk of the Catholic Church. . . . Any universal constitution to which we might approach, would be ultimately of the federalist type.[13]

The groups of groups, the catholic church, was thus highly organic and disorganised.[14] Consequently Figgis remarked: 'We stand, in brief, for the social and federal idea in the Church against a doctrine which is as autocratic as a Caliphate. . . . That is the issue between England and Rome.'[15] Ultimately no one part of the church, no one source of authority, could ever claim itself to be *the* catholic church.[16]

Any theory of authority, be it political or ecclesiastical, had to take account of the massive changes which had been experienced in the modern world. The medieval view of the state as a community of communities (*communitas communitatum*) had been definitively destroyed by the Reformation, which, according to Figgis, 'at once expressed and intensified the belief in the inherent sanctity of civil government in the Divine Right of Kings'.[17] In turn systems of government which emerged from the Reformation required coercive police powers which ultimately derived their authority from the divine right of kings; at the same time, such authority was characterised theologically in terms of a particular understanding of exclusiveness, absoluteness and truth. For Figgis, such a system had never in practice worked, but came about through what he called the 'cardinal error of identifying authority with the policeman'.[18]

Out of this theory emerged what Figgis regarded as the twin Reformation despots of the sovereign state and the sovereign church, both of which at different times claimed to possess all authority both temporal and spiritual. Yet, as a somewhat ironic consequence, Figgis regarded the division of Christendom itself as the first stage in the breakdown of this absolutist culture: there was more than one claim on absolute truth. Though each might claim a divine right, the very existence of two competing divine rights implied that either one system was wrong, or alternatively that a means of coexistence (pluralism) had to be devised.

For Figgis, then, what was of crucial importance in the emergence of the modern world was the coexistence of more than one church. Even though each church might claim an exclusive possession of the truth, the fact of plurality forced a degree of toleration, however limited and repressive: thus however absolute its claims, religion was ultimately a matter of choice. As Norman Sykes put it (somewhat tastelessly) in relation to England: 'For better and for worse the Tudor theory of the identity of Church and State had been finally shattered; and the future pattern of English religious life was never to approach the ideal of *ein Reich, ein Volk, eine Kirche*.'[19]

Toleration, pluralism and the modern church

The English Act of Toleration, according to Figgis, 'was bound to turn Christendom into a mere section of mankind'.[20] As soon as there was a recognition of more than one claim to absolute truth, each church, including the established church, would simply be forced to give a certain degree of freedom to others. In this way, Figgis suggested, 'It was the competing claims of religious bodies, and the inability of any single one to destroy the others, which finally secured liberty.'[21] More bluntly, he suggested that such liberty 'does not mean the right to punch the heads of those who disagree with you'.[22] Thus all the church could hope for in the modern world was to become one group among many, since it was no longer possible (or even desirable) to impose the will of one particular society on the whole. This was 'tenable in theory only on the puritan or medieval notion of a State, and in practice as absurd as the proposal of John Knox to punish adultery with death'.[23] In a situation where toleration was practised, the sort of authority claimed by the church had to be consonant with some degree of pluralism: although there was inevitably a proclamation of a more or less exclusive truth by any church or sect, this was always tempered by the existence of other competing claims:

> We cannot claim liberty for ourselves, while at the same time proposing to deny it to others. If we are to cry 'hands off' to the civil power in regard to such matters as marriage, doctrine, ritual, or the conditions of communion inside the church – and it is the necessary condition of a free religious society that it should regulate these matters – then we must give up attempting to dictate the policy of the state in regard to the whole mass of its citizens.[24]

By becoming a voluntary community of like-minded and committed individuals the church would be able to free itself from tutelage to a particular ruling class, clerical or lay. In short, Figgis claimed: 'Conventional religion and polite unbelief are gone for ever. You cannot live as comfortably if you are a Christian as if you are not – so do not try.'[25]

The organisation of the church

Although Figgis's understanding of the church implied the recognition of pluralism, he was at the same time quite able to see the
church as retaining authoritative structures, since for any voluntary
group to exist it required boundaries and certain shared rules.[26] The
unbridled freedom to belong to a religious group, however, was frequently confused with the freedom *within* the religious group.[27]
This combination of pluralism and authority, which is the hallmark
of the voluntary group and a pluralist politics, created something of
a paradox. Figgis tried to overcome the difficulty by viewing the
authority of the church as always relative to the individual's conscious act of voluntary submission. Thus, against many of his
contemporaries, Figgis held that all infallible authority, whether in
the church or in the state, was in its essence merely an extension of
the medieval idea of sovereignty and had been superseded in the
modern world. Instead, the concept of voluntary commitment
meant that the coercive authority of the church, and any absolute
authority it claimed, was severely curtailed despite all claims to
infallibility and absoluteness, since any power it retained could no
longer be identified with the police powers of the state, but was
always relative to the decision of the individual to accept voluntary
constraints.

Ultimately, then, authority derived not from any particular institution, but from the individual's decision to accept something or
somebody as authoritative through joining the group. In a rather
parochial Cambridge example Figgis likens this form of authority
to that found in the rowing eight, where each member of the crew
is as vital as all the others and where each contributes his or her
own part. Authority, on this model, is at once both external and
internal to the individual, since in making a conscious decision to
agree to abide by a set of external rules, the individual also to some
extent externalises his or her internal decision: 'The ultimate basis
of all authority, whether religious or political, and even educational or aesthetic, is the fact that no man is complete in himself;
that man is a social being.'[28]

The individual, in joining a group, thus accepts a certain external form of authority, but such external authority is necessarily
related to the decision of the individual in the act of submission in
the first place. In turn the group exerts a very real influence over
the individual. The group thus functions as a 'person with a mind

and will of its own'[29] analogous to that of the state. This close inter-connection between external and internal authority meant that 'the one inalienable note' of authority was that '[all] alike share in [it], all in some way submit to it, and all in some way contribute to it'.[30]

In summary, then, Figgis saw all authority in the church (which could be said of any other voluntary group and even of the state) as related vitally to the individuals who comprised it. Similarly no body within the church could set itself up as the ultimate law-giving authority over and above the members of the group: 'Church authority,' Figgis held, 'is a communal fact in which every single member – not the priests or the bishops alone – has his part.'[31] Most crucially for the development of a pluralist politics, authority was thus not about passive acquiescence to an external sovereign but was instead derived from an active participation intimately bound up with the decision to join the group. If the temptation towards passive submission was not going to win the day, there had to be a continual reminder that in the end each individual conscience must decide for itself:

> What we most need to realise is that authority in the Church of God is the expression of the life of the whole Christian community, and no single member but plays his part. Of all dangers which beset the statement of the idea of authority, none at this moment is so serious as that which views it purely as external command. The moment that notion is accepted, we are far on the way to the notion that the duty of the majority is merely passive.[32]

The limits of the state

At the same time as outlining the boundaries of the authority of the church, Figgis also attempted to circumscribe the limits of the authority which was to be ascribed to the state. Although the church had more or less been forced to accept its changed role in modern society, and had *de facto* recognised its similarity to other voluntary groups, the same could not be said of the state. The consequences of tolerance and pluralism may have been recognised by the church, but the state appeared to know no limits to its authority. Indeed, in England the deified authority granted to the king had been retained in a bizarre hangover from the Middle Ages which had become embodied in the theory of parliamentary sovereignty and executive action:

> Englishmen, however, would do well to remember that the present fashion is to preach this doctrine of blind obedience, not to an infallible Church or a gilded autocrat, but to a non-representative Parliament and a jerrymandering administration. Whether, however, the doctrine of omnipotence be proclaimed in Church or State, whether it take the form of monarchy by Divine Right or the sovereignty of the people, always and everywhere the doctrine is false; for whether or no men can frame a logical theory to express the fact, the great fact at the root of all human society is that man is a person, a spiritual being; and that no power – not even a religious society – is absolute, but in the last resort his allegiance to his own conscience is final. In regard, moreover, to the Church, we cannot often enough repeat that the Church of the future must be a laymen's church (although it still must have its priesthood), that is, the great democracy of God's servants and Christ's brethren, and no exclusive or illimitable power into which they may look.[33]

Whether the foe was sovereignty or infallibility the consequences were the same. The enslavement to a body above law, above participation, meant that there was no control by the group on the power of the institution. And with regard to the state, the principle of conscious voluntary submission was denied as an authority previously underpinned by belief in a divine anointing was usurped by a parliament which claimed to base its authority on popular support.

Freedom and authority

In his discussion of the nature and function of the church in modern society, Figgis outlines the conception of a group in which authority is voluntarily accepted, such authority being derived from the very act of acceptance without relying on any notion of universally shared moral norms. There is no such thing as the common good, even though members of each group might well hold that their good ought to be common for all others. In its essence this is a doctrine of fraternity, or, as Figgis put it, a 'loyalty to the brotherhood of human life . . . a society springing out of loyalty to Christ the Redeemer'.[34] Within such a society there was an attempt to reconcile the claims of the autonomous individual with the need for this individual to be embedded in the group. Such a balance was evidently difficult since '[l]iberty and authority . . . seem able neither to live with one another nor without one another'.[35] It is thus not surprising that in 1907 Figgis should have been attracted to join the Community of the Resurrection, which in many ways was an experiment in this balance between individuality and group life, and which he felt would free him from an economic order 'which he had increasingly felt to be characteristic of a Babylon under doom'.[36]

Figgis attempted to formulate a doctrine of the church based on the understanding of autonomy and of pluralism which emerged after the breakdown of the Reformation settlement. Such an attempt to root autonomy within the group was something shared by many of the theologians active in other countries during the early years of the last century. Yet it was only Figgis who attempted to explore the full ecclesiological dimensions of this social thinking and, more importantly, to balance fraternity and community with pluralism and freedom. Figgis's achievement was thus to give a vision of the church which was consonant with the achievement of freedom, but which did not alienate the individual from the group. In Figgis the voluntary church which emerged after toleration thereby became the fraternal church in a pluralist society.

With this ecclesiological dimension Figgis went further than any of the other group theorists of the Edwardian period. Although Harold Laski was profoundly indebted to Figgis for many of his views on the relationship of the individual to society,[37] Figgis retained a religious basis for fraternity, claiming that it could never survive merely as a purely secular theory: 'Ultimately the doctrine of . . . Brotherhood will not be maintained apart from the Christian faith.'[38] In his realisation that living in groups as brothers and sisters is rooted in a Christian vision, Figgis provided a theological basis for a pluralist society.

The way forward

Those who seek to revive political pluralism or 'associationalism' as a credible model for the future would do well to remember that voluntarism requires a commitment to the group and a tempering of the rights of the individual by the demands of the group. The danger, however, is that the group will destroy the individual. To retain fraternity balanced with pluralism requires both an ethics of belonging, and also a participative democracy to ensure that the group does not annihilate individuality or the rights of other groups. This is the political equivalent to what Figgis calls the lay-men's church, and it seems to me to offer an important corrective to the 'common good' policies of the Blair government. However, both fraternity and participation can only be achieved by a funda-mental reorientation not merely of the structures of society but also of the participants of that society. To see the state as the means of integration is both a dangerous and an anti-pluralist attempt to circumvent the very principles of participative democracy. Instead, for the pluralist, the state preserves the rights of groups, arbitrates in disputes, ensures that the weak and powerless can participate in decision-making, but importantly it does not lead with its own agenda or seek to define the 'common good'. Instead, that is left for the players to argue over.

Building on Figgis's theory it would seem that if voluntarism and participation become the basis for society (as well as for the church and any other group), then some of the problems of community as well as centralism and managerialism might begin to be overcome. Furthermore, participation can be encouraged since commitment to the group will be the way in which the society can be changed: democracy becomes far more direct and localised. It will make a difference whether or not one belongs: a participative democracy encourages an ethics of belonging and a sense that decisions can be shaped by commitment to the group. Voluntary, participative asso-ciation becomes the foundation for authority in society rather than any 'right to rule' imposed from above. States exist principally to prevent the competing groups coming to blows.

Once again, however, the problem emerges of how to ensure that the group does not annihilate individuality, and most especially the individuality of those in other groups, especially minority groups. The role of the state is to prevent the universal claims of any community, to prevent the right of any group to define the com-mon good. The state's role is to ensure the full participation of competing groups and to equalise the distribution of resources and power, which in turn requires a commitment to pluralism, that is the rights of others to exist as different. As Paul Hirst has convincingly shown, such a system, which he calls 'associationalism', can become a coherent and economically efficient means of organising welfare and social provision.[39] Similarly, it might increase involvement and overcome something of the alienation and lawlessness of modern society: a say in decision-making is conferred on all groups, but it is a process that does not shun conflict in the name of a premature harmony.

And in this it bears a similarity to some of the stakeholder ideas introduced, under Frank Field's influence, into various government activities (like, for instance, the 'primary care trusts' which consist of different stakeholders in health provision). What is as yet untested, however, is the level of popular participation in such new institutions. Expertise, confidentiality and vested interest, as well as appointment by patronage, create very real difficulties for reform of mass bureaucracies. Associationalism would mean far more thoroughgoing forms of democratic accountability and participation. This points to the need for radical devolution, not simply the reduplication of quasi-nation states with power devolved from above, but a reorientation to the periphery, where participation can begin to bite and where life-shaping decisions can be made.

The failures of the past are clear: on the one hand, a socialism which tries to enforce equality or fraternity untempered by liberty quickly collapses into either a virtual dictatorship by the ruling minority (which is the obvious danger of communitarianism), or it degenerates into state socialism (the danger of centralist models of authority), or it leads to inefficient, alienating and virtually unaccountable bureaucracies (as with the welfare consensus). On the other hand, liberty unbalanced by fraternity can easily fall prey to the sinister influences of aristocracy, or the anarchy of the market. Or it can lead to a meaningless rhetoric which in practice offers little more than an amoral centralised statism protecting a small sectional interest (as with Mrs Thatcher).[40]

In distinction, a society constructed through an amalgam of groups – traditionally the guilds and the friendly societies[41] – suggests a pluralism based on the need to coexist: different groups have different purposes, but are voluntary organisations functioning to deliver certain goods or services. The state has no sovereignty except that delegated to it from below for its role in policing the competing groups and ensuring a just and equitable distribution of access to decision-making and resources. Devolution is not from the centre to the periphery, but from the periphery to the centre: consequently the principle of associationalism and voluntarism requires a far more thoroughgoing reform than Frank Field has imagined. Instead of changing people's characters, associationalists conceive a participative system of democracy beyond that of the stakeholder. It is not that people are to be given a stake in their welfare provision or in the workings of society: instead they are to be given *all* the reins of power which is then to be delegated upwards when needs be or when there are conflicting claims. The role of the state, particularly as the guardian or regenerator of the nation's morals, consequently disappears.

But it gains a new role, as guardian of the constitution (the right to have a say in decision-making, whatever one's background) and the right to be different. Despite this constitutional recognition of pluralism and difference, particular participative groups, e.g. churches and political parties, may well hold strong moral views and they might well feel that what they say has universal significance. To survive, however, no one group will be able to arbitrate for all other groups. In practice, this means that morality can no longer be considered as universalisable. The role of the state is thus to ensure that no group universalises its goals to the exclusion of others: and that requires legal protection and economic support for the weak, as well as an institutionalised system of conflict resolution (which would strengthen parliament at the expense of the executive). There is not space here to work out the details of such a system: suffice it to say that it is an as yet untested possibility. But what is needed now is work on practicalities. As Paul Hirst writes: 'Whether associationalism can act as a supplement to our failing institutions now depends not on restating the principle, but on working out the detail of credible models of associational governance in the economy and welfare sectors.'[42]

The possibility of living with others, and of being in conflict, implies that our group might just possibly be wrong and we might possibly have something to learn by engaging with other groups. How this is to be achieved is an open question. But a tentative (if pragmatic) answer might be this: if I don't hit you then perhaps you won't hit me. The role left for the state is to ensure that neither of us hits one another, or if we do, then it should stop us repeating our action and help us reconcile or live with our differences. In Figgis's ecclesiology, the catholic church is an international peacekeeper, and its authority derives solely from the need to settle disputes. If by analogy the state is much the same, then it has no sovereignty except that delegated to it from below for this particular function. 'Subsidiarity' (another concept developed from the conciliarist thinking of the Middle Ages) is not, for Figgis, a devolution of power from the top down, but a commitment to peace-keeping from the bottom up. And what this shows is that conflict can be a better guarantee of peace than premature consensus. Yet, again, how that works in practice is another question.

Communities with a say in decision-making will be quite unlike the servile communities of civil society. Voluntary communities can undoubtedly help in counterbalancing the claims and sovereignty of the state. As Ernest Gellner put it: 'whilst not preventing the state from fulfilling its role of keeper of the peace and arbitrator between major interests, [the institutions of civil society] can nevertheless prevent the state from dominating and atomizing the rest of society'.[43] However, to function as anything more than groups which fulfil the purpose of integrating people in the status quo, the voluntary communities of civil society need enough power to be able to threaten the dominion of the state and to question the values of the executive: people are only likely to participate in such organisations if they are capable of changing things. In turn, participatory democracy becomes important within the voluntary institution itself: the recent history of the National Trust in its disputes over hunting provides a good example. To some extent, it has changed from an organisation with a passive membership to one whose members are active and participatory. When this happens governments begin to take notice. At the public level, participatory or stakeholder (rather than government) audit might well be a model worth exploring.

Furthermore, there is no obvious reason why the principles of community should be limited to the voluntary sector. Indeed, it seems quite extraordinary that the workplace is exempted from the values of community in most of the rhetoric. A revival of the idea of functionalist democracy, pioneered with the Whitley Report at the end of the first world war, could transform social relationships and participation. It will be interesting to see if some of the new government initiatives (like Network Rail or foundation hospitals) have the courage and vision to realise Harold Laski's tantalising idea of giving workplace groups real power against the supposed sovereignty of the omnicompetent state. As he put it in 1921: 'The railways are as real as Lancashire; and exactly as the specifically local problems of Lancashire are dealt with by it, so could the specifically local problems of the railways be dealt with by a governing body of its own.'[44] A massive increase in the principle of democratic governance, with partnerships of users, workers and owners, could give the non-governmental sector a real clout (but would at the same time threaten the oligarchic 'right to manage' and other such undemocratic slogans). This would be to take the stakeholder idea seriously.[45] In this way, democracy would become an all-pervasive activity exercised by participation in different places by different people in many different communities. Democracy would extend throughout society, and would not be simply confined to the occasional general election. But once again the sovereign power of the executive would be threatened.

Partnerships would develop and, although this might merely be wishful thinking, suspicion might be overcome in new relationships of trust. On such a system, sovereignty would be dispersed, and the state would function as a kind of equaliser and regulator, but would not be overly anxious about taking the initiative in building moral communities at all.[46] Federalism would not be a matter of concession, i.e. top downwards (which is presumably why Scotland does not have a Prime Minister but only a 'First' Minister), but of *necessity*, as sovereignty and values are dispersed throughout the different participatory bodies ('communities') within the state. In this way pluralist democracy would be guaranteed through communicative negotiation.[47] After all, there seems to be little evidence in the United Kingdom of a new moral consensus, but far more evidence of value pluralism and communal difference, often fostered by faith communities. The racial tensions in Oldham and Bradford present obvious recent examples. It may be, however, that rather than fostering a new moral consensus, a healthy society will be one that promotes what Ralf Dahrendorf called a 'creative chaos'. Indeed, the role of government might be better understood as ensuring creative communication between different participatory groups, rather than government seeing itself as some kind of an agency whose role is to set the moral agenda. In such a state there would be many values from many communities, many common goods, but no single set of 'values of community' and no common good. And it may be that there is little justification for the claim that the state's role is to promote the good life, when there is no clear consensus as to what that good life might consist of. As Laski put it aphoristically: 'A community that cannot agree is a community capable of advance.'[48]

For the Christian, it is good to reflect along with Figgis on the fact that medieval society had no highly developed theory of the state or of sovereignty, but was composed instead of many intermediate organisations:[49] there is no particular reason why it should be impossible to change things now, and the advantage of the pluralist proposals made in this chapter is that they are gradualist and experimental. Instead of the often woolly talk that clamours for moral communities, it might be better to moralise those we already have: and that would be to change the cult of managerialism founded on a 'heresthetic rhetoric' as outlined in Chapter 3, as well as the centralisation of sovereignty in the executive, and to renegotiate the legitimacy of executive government. But it would also be to reinvigorate democracy as all people might be re-enfranchised as moral agents in all aspects of their lives (instead of simply every five years, or in the evenings and at the weekends). And such a vision might also promote a new sense of trust and hope, which is what is needed in any well-functioning society.[50]

It is precisely at this point, however, that Christian values return. To function, as J. N. Figgis recognised,[51] the pluralism of a participative, associationalist democracy requires a commitment to the intrinsic value of difference, as well as the humility to live alongside those with whom one is in disagreement. Indeed, such pluralism, one might claim, is the social embodiment of the recognition that all have sinned and fall short of the glory of God. Quite simply, no one group has access to the 'common good', not even the Christian church (and even less Frank Field's clerisy or the self-appointed guardians of the moral quangos). And if pluralism is a Christian theory, at least in origin, then it would not seem out of place for Christians to work out a programme for reform of sovereignty instead of retreating into their communitarian ghettos which leave the state untouched or becoming defenders of the status quo. Consequently, I would suggest, Christians have much to contribute to social thought, but only after they have learnt to value pluralism, for it is at the heart of the Christian doctrine of humanity. Anything else – and that includes the 'common good' – seems to be Pelagian, to deny the fact that we might have erred and might be wrong. The tragedy for the modern world is that few communities and even fewer states are able to recognise their own frailty. Christian politics, if it is to be Christian, needs to learn the limits of human certainty and how to legislate for such conditions. And, one might suggest, neither modesty nor lack of absolute certainty have as yet been tested in the political domain. Theories of absolute sovereignty are far more enticing.

So by way of conclusion let me return to Tony Blair's vision:

> People live in communities. I think of Britain as a community of citizens with common needs, mutual interests, shared objectives, related goals and most of all linked destinies.[52]

One needs to ask whether this New Britain envisioned by Tony Blair is a Britain which is pluralist, diverse and which values difference and where all are called on to participate in the political process, or whether the new community is just another effort to bolster a flagging state in an increasingly fragmented, market-led and individualist world through the dangerous rhetoric of national unity and objective morality. The jury, it seems to me, is still out on this matter. Just how pluralist are Blair's shared objectives, and linked destinies?

The New Labour project is being tested in the harsh conditions of political reality: it has encountered crisis, failure and most recently war. The rhetoric is tempered by the constraints of practice. My question is whether the language of community, which seems to stem from a particular kind of Christianity (albeit one with serious shortcomings), is the only solution to Christian politics. It is crucial to note that there are many different types of Christianity, not all of which will be quite so certain of the common good and shared objectives. The humility of the pluralist vision, which, at least on Figgis's account, stems from the medieval anti-papalist conciliarist tradition,[53] stands in marked contrast to the moralism of other versions of Christianity. Indeed, so many of these seem to rest on the utter certainty of revealed law (even when such a law seems as benign as the common good). Christian politicians would do well to look closely at their Christianity. It is not clear to me that it need necessarily elevate (or even recognise) the sovereignty of the state, or, for that matter, allow us to glimpse the common good. And if they do that, then they might start to make a contribution to a tolerant, open and conversational state, or, to put it another way, to a truly Christian form of politics.

1. The Old and the New

1. Mervyn Stockwood, *The Cross and the Sickle* (London: Sheldon Press, 1978).
2. On the history and politics of this period see Stephen Driver and Luke Martell, *Blair's Britain* (Cambridge: Polity, 2002), esp. chs 1 and 2, and Jeremy Black, *Britain Since the Seventies: Politics and Society in the Consumer Age* (London: Reaktion Books, 2004).
3. Tony Blair, *New Britain. My Vision of a Young Country* (London: Fourth Estate, 1996), p. 38.
4. Ibid., p. 50.
5. Statement agreed by the Labour Party NEC, 13 March 1995. On the struggles over modernisation and Clause Four, see Jon Sopel, *Tony Blair. The Moderniser* (London: Bantam, 1995), ch. 13.
6. Cf. C. A. R. Crosland, *The Future of Socialism* (London: Cape, 1956).
7. William Temple, *Christianity and Social Order* (Harmondsworth: Penguin, 1942).
8. Ibid., p. 73.
9. Temple coined the term as early as 1928. See Matthew Grimley, *Citizenship, Community, and the Church of England* (Oxford: Clarendon, 2004), p. 1.
10. Temple, *Christianity and Social Order*, p. 75.
11. Ibid., p. 75.
12. A brilliant critique of Temple's assumptions is offered by David Nicholls in *Deity and Domination* (London: Routledge, 1989), pp. 48–50.
13. See esp. the Appendix to *Christianity and Social Order*, pp. 75–90.
14. Temple, *Christianity and Social Order*, pp. 62–6.
15. See David Marquand, *Decline of the Public* (Cambridge: Polity, 2004), ch. 3.
16. Temple, *Christianity and Social Order*, p. 35.
17. William Temple, *The Education of Citizens* (London: Parents' National Educational Union, 1905), p. 5.
18. William Temple, *Christianity and the State* (London: Macmillan, 1928),

pp. 169–70; see also *Citizen and Churchman* (London: Eyre and Spottiswoode, 1941), pp. 26, 35.

2. Community

1. Ferdinand Tönnies, *Community and Civil Society*, translated by José Harris and M. Hollis (Cambridge: Cambridge University Press, 2001).
2. E. and S. Yeo, 'On the Uses of Community from Owenism to the Present' in Stephen Yeo (ed.), *New Views of Co-operation* (London: Routledge, 1988), pp. 229–58.
3. Tony Blair, *New Britain. My Vision of a Young Country* (London: Fourth Estate, 1996), p. 299.
4. Ibid., p. 308.
5. Ibid., pp. 308–9.
6. Ibid., p. 237.
7. Ibid., p. 121.
8. Ibid., p. 37.
9. Ibid., p. 39.
10. Tony Blair, 'Forging a New Agenda' in *Marxism Today* (October 1991), p. 32.
11. Cf. David Nicholls, *Deity and Domination* (London: Routledge, 1989) p. 49. See Matthew Grimley, *Citizenship, Community, and the Church of England* (Oxford: Clarendon, 2004), pp. 212–13.
12. John Macmurray, *Conditions of Freedom* (London: Faber, 1956), p. 56. Cf. *Persons In Relation* (London: Faber, 1961), esp. chs 6 and 7. See further, Chris Bryant, *Possible Dreams* (London: Hodder and Stoughton, 1996), ch. 8.
13. John Rentoul, *Tony Blair* (London: Warner Books, 1996), p. 45.
14. Blair, *New Britain*, pp. 238–9.
15. Tony Blair, 'Why I am a Christian', *Sunday Telegraph* (7 April 1996), Review Section, p. 1. It is interesting that it is only when it is annexed to the adjective 'Christian', and presumably moderated or neutered, that the word 'socialism' is acceptable to Tony Blair and his fellow cabinet members of the Christian Socialist Movement.
16. 'Values and the Power of Community'. Speech to the Global Ethics Foundation, Tübingen University, 30 June 2000.
17. Callum Brown, *The Death Of Christian Britain* (London: Routledge, 2001), p. 197.
18. See Grace Davie, *Religion in Modern Europe* (Oxford: Oxford University Press, 2000).
19. Andrew Vincent and Raymond Plant, *Philosophy, Politics and Citizenship* (Oxford: Blackwell, 1984), p. 165.
20. David Marquand, *Taming Leviathan: Social Democracy and Decentralisation* (London: Socialist Commentary Publications, 1980), p. 8.

21. See David Marquand's essay, 'Reinventing Civic Republicanism' in *The New Reckoning. Capitalism, States and Citizens* (Cambridge: Polity, 1997), pp. 37–52.

22. David Marquand, 'After Socialism' in *The New Reckoning*, pp. 53–70, here pp. 68–9.

23. David Marquand, *Decline of the Public* (Cambridge: Polity, 2004), esp. ch. 2.

24. On this see Wendy Wheeler, 'Dangerous Business' in Mark Perryman (ed.), *The Blair Agenda* (London: Lawrence and Wishart, 1996), pp. 100–24.

25. See Chris Coates, *Utopia Britannica: British Utopian Experiments: 1325–1945* (London: Diggers and Dreamers, 2001).

26. Blair's speech is at www.policy-network.net/php.

27. 'Remarks by the President at the closing session of the Conference on Progressive Governance', Berlin, 3 June 2000.

28. E.g. Anthony Giddens, *The Third Way. The Renewal of Social Democracy* (Cambridge: Polity, 1998), ch. 5. The term 'Third Way' has proved more popular in Germany. Giddens' book exists in German translation: *Der dritte Weg. Die Erneuerung der sozialen Demokratie* (Frankfurt-am-Main: Suhrkamp, 1999).

29. Speech to the annual conference of the NFWI, 7 June 2000.

30. Giddens, *The Third Way*.

31. Speech to the Labour Party Conference, 2 October 2001.

32. Speech to the Scottish Labour Party Conference, 22 February 2002.

33. Speech to the Labour Party Conference, 1 October 2002.

3. Management

1. W. H. Riker, *The Art of Political Manipulation* (New Haven: Yale University Press, 1986).

2. Iain McLean, *Rational Choice and British Politics. An Analysis of Rhetoric and Manipulation from Peel to Blair* (Oxford: Oxford University Press, 2001), p. 225.

3. Bank of England Act 1998.

4. Letter of 18 Jan 2000 at www.bankofengland.co.uk/mpc/buiterletter.htm.

5. Tony Blair, 'Values and the Power of Community', 30 June 2000.

6. On this, see Paul Hirst, *From Statism to Pluralism* (London: UCL Press, 1997), pp. 96–114.

7. On this, see Richard H. Roberts, *Religion, Theology and the Human Sciences* (Cambridge: Cambridge University Press, 2001).

8. H. J. Laski, *Authority in the Modern State* (New Haven: Yale University Press, 1919), p. 78.

9. On this, see John Gray, *False Dawn. The Delusions of Global Capitalism* (London: Granta, 1999), esp. ch. 2.

10. 'A Partial Response to My Critics' in John Horton and Susan Mendus (eds), *After MacIntyre* (Cambridge: Polity Press, 1994), pp. 283–304, here p. 303.

11. Paul Hirst, *Associative Democracy* (Cambridge: Polity. 1994), and *From Statism to Pluralism*; David Nicholls, *The Pluralist State* (London: Macmillan, 1975).

12. See Laski, *Authority in the Modern State*, p. 22; H. J. Laski, *Studies in the Problem of Sovereignty* (New Haven: Yale University Press, 1917), p. 2.

4. Theologies of Community and Theologies of Conflict

1. Conrad Noel, *Jesus The Heretic* (London: J. M. Dent, 1939), p. 46. On Noel, see Conrad Noel, *An Autobiography*, ed. Sydney Dark (London: J. M. Dent, 1945); Robert Woodifield, 'Conrad Noel' in Maurice B. Reckitt (ed.), *For Christ and People* (London: SPCK, 1968), pp. 135–79; Reg Groves, *Conrad Noel and the Thaxted Movement. An Adventure in Christian Socialism* (New York: Augustus M. Keeley, 1968); Mark D. Chapman, *Liturgy, Socialism and Life: The Legacy of Conrad Noel* (London: DLT, 2001).

2. Conrad Noel, *The Battle of the Flags. A Study in Christian Politics* (London: The Labour Publishing House, 1922), p. 56.

3. Ibid., p. 95.

4. Noel, *Jesus The Heretic*, p. 2.

5. Noel, *Battle of the Flags*, p. 95.

6. Noel, *Jesus the Heretic*, p. 219.

7. Kenneth Leech, *The Social God* (London: Sheldon Press, 1981), p. 6.

8. Ibid., p. 7. For a more recent statement of similar themes, see Kenneth Leech, *The Sky is Red* (London: DLT, 1997), e.g. pp. 33–7.

9. Leonardo Boff, *Trinity and Society* (Tunbridge Wells: Burns and Oates, 1988), p. 11.

10. Ibid., p. 15.

11. Ibid., p. 148.

12. Ibid., p. 151.

13. Ibid., p. 153.

14. Jürgen Moltmann, *The Trinity and the Kingdom of God* (London: SCM, 1981), p. 173.

15. Ibid., pp. 174, 199.

16. Ibid., p. 199.

17. Ibid., p. 198.

18. Ibid., p. 215.

19. Ibid., p. 197. The parallels with Noel are striking. For a critique, see

David Nicholls, *Deity and Domination* (London: Routledge, 1989), esp. p. 235.

20. Jürgen Moltmann, 'The Social Doctrine of the Trinity' in James Byrne (ed.), *The Christian Understanding of God Today* (Dublin: Columba, 1993), pp. 110–11.

21. Metropolitan Geevarghese Mar Osthathios, *Theology of a Classless Society* (Guildford: Lutterworth Press, 1979).

22. Ibid., p. 82.

23. Ibid., p. 45.

24. Ibid., p. 95.

25. Ibid., p. 68.

26. Ibid., p. 24.

27. Ibid., p. 74.

28. Colin Gunton, *The Promise of Trinitarian Theology* (Edinburgh: T & T Clark, 1993), p. 95.

29. John Zizioulas, *Being as Communion. Studies in Personhood and the Church* (London: DLT, 1985).

30. See, for example John Macmurray, *Persons in Relation* (London: Faber, 1961), p. 60: 'human experience is, in principle shared experience; human life even in its most individual elements is a common life'. For Gunton's discussion of Macmurray, see *The Promise of Trinitarian Theology*, esp. pp. 90–2.

31. Gunton, *The Promise of Trinitarian Theology*, p. 9, citing *Being as Communion*, p. 17.

32. Ibid., p. 12. See also pp. 73–5.

33. Colin Gunton, *The One, The Three and the Many. God, Creation and the Culture of Modernity* (Cambridge: Cambridge University Press, 1993), p. 124.

34. Ibid., p. 125.

35. Ibid., p. 229.

36. Ibid., p. 223.

37. Thomas D. Parker, 'The Political Meaning of the Doctrine of the Trinity: some theses' in *Journal of Religion* 60 (1980), pp. 165–84, here pp. 179, 182.

38. George Lindbeck, *The Nature of Doctrine: Religion and Theology in a Postliberal Age* (London: SPCK, 1984), p. 107.

39. Rowan Williams, 'The Literal Sense of Scripture' in *Modern Theology* 7 (1991), pp. 121–34, here p. 132.

40. Paul S. Fiddes, *Participating in God. A Pastoral Doctrine of the Trinity* (London: DLT, 2000).

41. James Mackey, 'Are There Christian Alternatives to Trinitarian Thinking?' in *The Christian Understanding of God Today*, pp. 66–75, here p. 71.

42. David Nicholls, 'Trinity and Conflict', in *Theology* XCVI (1993), pp. 19–27, here p. 26. See also *Deity and Domination*, esp. p. 239.
43. Nicholls, 'Trinity and Conflict', p. 19.
44. Jürgen Moltmann, *The Crucified God* (London: SCM, 1974), esp. p. 245.
45. Cf. Nicholls, *Deity and Domination*, p. 239.
46. Nicholls, 'Trinity and Conflict', p. 24.
47. Ibid., p. 26.
48. Nicholls, *Deity and Domination*, pp. 239–40.

5. Community and Pluralism

1. On the crisis in Edwardian England see my book, *The Coming Crisis: The Impact of Eschatology on Edwardian England* (Sheffield: Sheffield Academic Press, 2001).
2. Mark D. Chapman, 'Theology, Nationalism and the First World War: Christian Ethics and the Constraints of Politics' in *Studies in Christian Ethics* 8 (1995), pp. 13–35.
3. Roland N. Stromberg, *Redemption by War. The Intellectuals and 1914* (Lawrence: Regent's Press of Kansas, 1982), p. 198.
4. On this and the abiding importance of nationalism, see the somewhat pessimistic revisions to the second edition of Eric Hobsbawm, *Nations and Nationalism: Programme, Myth, Reality* (Cambridge: Cambridge University Press, 1992), ch. 6, esp. p. 192.
5. On this, see David Coates and Joel Krieger, *Blair's War* (Cambridge: Polity, 2004), esp. chs 3 and 4. Quotation cited on p. 58.
6. See his address to the nation of 21 March 2003 (the outbreak of war), cited in *Blair's War*, pp. 61–2.
7. *The Alternative Service Book*, 1980, p. 125; *Common Worship*, p. 281.
8. In *Hymns Old and New: Complete Anglican Edition*, no. 224.
9. See also David Nicholls, *Deity and Domination* (London: Routledge, 1989), p. 52.
10. 'Blair's Moral Crusade' in the *Observer*, 5 September 1999, pp. 8–9.
11. See also Derek Philips, *Looking Backward: A Critical Appraisal of Communitarian Thought* (Princeton: Princeton University Press, 1993). For an overview of communitarianism (written in dialogical form), see Daniel Bell, *Communitarianism and its Critics* (Oxford: Clarendon Press, 1993).
12. See Andrew Whiteford and Michael McGrath, *The Distribution of Income in South Africa* (Pretoria: Human Sciences Research Council, 1994), table 5.1.
13. For the official statements on the Moral Regeneration Movement, see the South African Government website at www.gov.za/issues/mrm/index.html.

14. On this see David Hollenbach SJ, *The Common Good and Christian Ethics* (Cambridge: Cambridge University Press, 2003), esp. ch. 2.

15. Cited at www.dac.gov.za/news/speeches/2002_04_16.htm.

16. In conversations with large numbers of black clergy in Cape Town and Johannesburg in June 2003, it was notable how frequently I was asked about the problem of maintaining the Church's identity in a democratic state.

17. Hobsbawm, *Nations and Nationalism*, pp. 9–13.

6. Communities, Civil Society and the Reconstruction of Politics

1. Jonathan Sacks, *The Persistence of Faith* (London: Weidenfeld and Nicolson, 1992).

2. Gerhard Lohfink, *Jesus and Community: The Social Dimension of Christian Faith* (Philadelphia: Fortress, 1984).

3. Gordon White, 'Civil Society, Democratization and Development' in *Democratization* I (1994), pp. 375–90, here p. 379.

4. Amitai Etzioni, *The Spirit of Community: Rights, Responsibility and the Communitarian Agenda* (New York: Crown, 1993).

5. Adam B. Seligman, *The Problem of Trust* (Princeton: Princeton University Press, 1997); Anthony Giddens, *The Third Way. The Renewal of Social Democracy* (Cambridge: Polity, 1998).

6. Jürgen Habermas, *Autonomy and Solidarity* (London: Verso, 1992), p. 47.

7. Alasdair MacIntyre, *After Virtue* (London: Duckworth, 1981).

8. See Sacks, *The Persistence of Faith*.

9. Robin Gill, *Moral Communities* (Exeter: Exeter University Press, 1992).

10. Cited in Tony Blair, *New Britain. My Vision of a Young Country* (London: Fourth Estate, 1996), p. 239.

11. On Frank Field, see Alan Deacon, 'Self Interest and Collective Welfare: Frank Field and the Debate about the Future of Work' in Andrew R. Morton (ed.), *The Future of Welfare* (Edinburgh: Centre for Theology and Public Issues, 1997), pp. 119–32. See also the responses by Duncan Forrester ('Welfare and Conviction Politics', pp. 133–40) and Frank Field ('Response to Alan Deacon', pp. 141–53) in the same work.

12. David Willetts, *Blair's Gurus* (London: Centre for Policy Studies, 1996), p. 31.

13. Frank Field, 'What Then Was Unthinkable?' in *Crucible* 38 (1999), pp. 16–30, here p. 16.

14. Frank Field, *Making Welfare Work. Reconstructing Welfare for the Millennium* (London: Institute of Community Studies, 1995), p. 129.

15. Field, *Making Welfare Work*, p. 122. Cf. 'What Then Was Unthinkable?', esp. p. 29.

16. Field, *Making Welfare Work*, p. 2.

17. Frank Field, *Freedom and Wealth in a Socialist Future* (London: Constable, 1987), p. 14.

18. In 'Welfare and Conviction Politics', Forrester notes, however, that Tawney never stressed self-interest 'as the main motive of social action in the way Field increasingly does' (p. 137).

19. Frank Field, 'Rejoinder' in Alan Deacon (ed.), *Stakeholder Welfare* (London: IEA, 1996), p. 108.

20. Field, 'Rejoinder', p. 107. On Tawney and Titmuss, see Ronald Preston, *Religion and the Persistence of Capitalism* (London: SCM Press, 1979) and Alan Deacon, 'Self Interest', pp. 128–9. See also 'Frank Field's Response to Alan Deacon', p. 151: 'I see the Titmuss legacy as establishing a post-war orthodoxy which, while beneficial in the age of the ration book, became an intellectual, political and moral cul-de-sac into which Labour was manoeuvred during so much of the latter post-war period.'

21. Cf. Forrester, 'Welfare and Conviction Politics', p. 136.

22. Field, 'What Then Was Unthinkable?', pp. 24, 23.

23. Ibid., p. 27.

24. See also the speech by Frank Field, 'Welfare: The Third Way' to the Consolidated Financial Insurance, 24 September 1997.

25. Frank Field, *An Agenda for Britain* (London: HarperCollins, 1993).

26. Ibid., p. 142.

27. Ibid., pp. 20–1.

28. Barbara Wootton, *In a World I Never Made* (London: Allen and Unwin, 1967), p. 279. Cited in *Freedom and Wealth in a Socialist Future*, p. 263.

29. Frank Field, *The Politics of Paradise. A Christian Approach to the Kingdom* (London: Fount, 1987).

30. Ibid., p. 31.

31. Ibid., p. 37.

32. Ibid., p. 54.

33. Ibid., p. 74.

34. Ibid.

35. See ibid., pp. 92–3. For a criticism of Frank Field's understanding of character, see Alan Deacon, 'Self-interest and Collective Welfare', esp. p. 125.

36. Field, *The Politics of Paradise*, p. 103.

37. Ibid., p. 129.

38. Ibid., p. 137.

39. See Frank Field, 'Socialism and the Politics of Radial Distribution' in David Ormrod (ed.), *Fellowship, Freedom and Equality. Lectures in Memory of R. H. Tawney* (London: Christian Socialist Movement, 1990), pp. 49–58.

40. Tony Benn, 'The Moral Basis of the Radical Left' in David Ormrod (ed.), *Fellowship, Freedom and Equality*, pp. 103–9, here p. 109.

7. Another Christian Politics: Pluralist Democracy

1. Most importantly by the late David Nicholls in *The Pluralist State* (London and Basingstoke: Macmillan, second edition, 1994) and Paul Hirst in several books: *The Pluralist Theory of the State* (London: Routledge, 1989), *Associative Democracy* (Cambridge: Polity Press, 1994) and *From Statism to Pluralism* (London: UCL Press, 1997). See also the earlier works by K. C. Hsaio, *Political Pluralism* (London: Kegan Paul, 1927); and H. M. Magid, *English Political Pluralism* (New York: Columbia University Press, 1941). On the demise of guild socialism and political pluralism, see S. T. Glass, *The Responsible Society* (London: Longmans, 1966). For a brief summary of pluralist thought see Matthew Grimley, *Citizenship, Community and the Church of England*, ch. 2.

2. His lectures were published as *From Gerson to Grotius* (Cambridge: Cambridge University Press, 1907).

3. Figgis seems to have enjoyed his period as a parish priest, devoting much time to visiting and to entertaining his parishioners. There are many stories of his wit, his absent-mindedness and his boyish laugh. See Maurice G. Tucker, *John Neville Figgis. A Study* (London: SPCK, 1950), pp. 12–15.

4. J. N. Figgis, *The Gospel and Human Needs* (London: Longmans, 1909).

5. See J. N. Figgis, *Antichrist and Other Sermons* (London: Longmans, 1913).

6. The only lengthy biographical account is Tucker, *John Neville Figgis*. See also the scanty sketch by Walter Frere in *DNB*, 1912–1921 and the anonymous obituary in the *Guardian*, 24 April, 1919, p. 430. There is much useful biographical information, especially on Figgis at Mirfield, in Alan Wilkinson, *The Community of the Resurrection. A Centenary History* (London: SCM, 1992).

7. This letter to F. C. Burkitt is written on Marnhull Rectory notepaper and is therefore before 1907 (Cambridge University Library MS Add 7658 B. 314).

8. J. N. Figgis, *Civilisation at the Cross Roads*, Four Lectures delivered before Harvard University in the year 1911 on the William Belden Noble Foundation (London: Longmans, 1912), p. ix.

9. Figgis, *Civilisation*, p. 34. Figgis is well aware of the critiques of moral philosophers like G. E. Moore, and the 'new realists' like Bertrand Russell (p. 41).

10. Borthwick Institute, York, Mirfield Deposit 3, Box 1, Notebook 2: lectures at University College, November 1912 and Leeds, November 1913 on political thought of the Middle Ages.

11. Figgis, *From Gerson to Grotius*, p. 2.

12. On this see my essay, 'Concepts of the Voluntary Church in England and Germany, 1890–1920: A Study of J. N. Figgis and Ernst Troeltsch' in *Zeitschrift für neuere Theologiegeschichte* 2 (1995), pp. 37–59.

13. J. N. Figgis, *Churches in the Modern State* (London: Longmans, 1914), pp. 165–6.

14. The appealing political interpretation of this ecclesiology has been developed by both Nicholls (in *The Pluralist State*, esp. chs 6 and 7) and Hirst (in *Associative Democracy*, ch. 7). The importance of a 'Europe of the regions' is stressed by Hirst in *From Statism to Pluralism*, passim.

15. Figgis, *Antichrist*, p. 137.

16. J. N. Figgis, *Hopes for English Religion* (London: Longmans, 1919), p. 75.

17. J. N. Figgis, 'Political Thought in the Sixteenth Century', in *Cambridge Modern History*, III, ed. Lord Acton (Cambridge: Cambridge University Press, 1904), pp. 736–69, here p. 759. See also 'Erastus and Erastianism' in *Journal of Theological Studies* 2 (1901).

18. Figgis, *Hopes*, p. 97.

19. N. P. Sykes, *The English Religious Tradition* (London: SCM, 1953), p. 44.

20. J. N. Figgis, *The Fellowship of the Mystery* (London: Longmans, 1914), pp. 90–1.

21. Figgis, *Churches in the Modern State*, p. 101.

22. Ibid., p. 120.

23. Ibid., pp. 123–4.

24. Ibid., pp. 112–13.

25. Figgis, *Gospel and Human Needs*, p. 152.

26. See Figgis, *Fellowship*, p. 181.

27. Ibid., pp. 184–5.

28. Figgis, *Antichrist*, p. 152. In an address on friendship, Figgis claimed that 'we are social beings, and it is in social and communal life that we find our own individuality' (unpublished address 'You are my friends' in Borthwick Institute, Mirfield Deposit 3, Box 3, Notebook 5).

29. Figgis, *Churches in the Modern State*, p. 99. On the concept of a 'group personality', see Nicholls, *The Pluralist State*, ch. 4.

30. Figgis, *Fellowship*, p. 189.

31. Figgis, *Hopes*, p. 38.

32. Figgis, *Fellowship*, p. 193.

33. Figgis, *Churches in the Modern State*, pp. 154–5. On this see esp. Hirst, *Associative Democracy*, chs 1 and 2.

34. Figgis, *Hopes*, p. 24.

35. Ibid., p. 114.

36. G. P. H. Pawson CR, *Edward Keble Talbot. His Community and His Friends* (London: SPCK, 1954), p. 53.

37. See Michael Newman, *Harold Laski. A Political Biography* (Basingstoke: Macmillan, 1993), pp. 38–9.

38. Figgis, *Hopes*, p. 136.

39. See esp. Hirst, *From Statism to Pluralism*, Part II.

40. John Gray, *False Dawn. The Delusions of Global Capitalism* (London: Granta, 1999), esp. pp. 23–38.

41. A good overview of the history of political theory from this perspective is Anthony Black, *Guild and State: European Political Thought from the Twelfth Century to the Present* (New Brunswick: Transaction, 2003).

42. Hirst, *From Statism to Pluralism*, p. 57.

43. Ernest Gellner, 'The Importance of Being Modular' in J. A. Hall (ed.), *Civil Society: Theory, History, Comparison* (Cambridge: Polity, 1995), pp. 32–55, here p. 32.

44. H. J. Laski, *The Foundations of Sovereignty and Other Essays* (London: Allen and Unwin, 1921), p. 70; see also *Authority in the Modern State* (New Haven: Yale University Press, 1919), p. 74.

45. Cf. Hirst, *Associative Democracy*, pp. 142–4.

46. Figgis, *Churches in the Modern State*, pp. 154–5.

47. Hirst, *Associative Democracy*, pp. 34–40; Jürgen Habermas, *The Theory of Communicative Action* (Cambridge: Polity, 1987).

48. Laski, *Studies in the Problem of Sovereignty*, p. 24; see also *Authority in the Modern State*, pp. 28, 67, 121. For a recent restatement of similar themes encapsulated in the notion of a *modus vivendi*, see John Gray, *Two Faces of Liberalism* (New York: New Press, 2000), ch. 4.

49. See also Otto von Gierke, *Political Theories of the Middle Ages* (Cambridge: Cambridge University Press, 1900).

50. Fran Tonkiss and Andrew Passey (eds), *Trust and Civil Society* (Basingstoke: Macmillan, 2000).

51. See his analysis of the conciliar movement in *From Gerson to Grotius*. For Figgis, political pluralism is fundamentally a secularised conciliarism.

52. Tony Blair, *Constitutional Change and the Future of Britain* (London: Charter 88 Trust, 1992), pp. 6–7.

53. See Figgis, *Churches in the Modern State*, p. 146.

BIBLIOGRAPHY

Daniel Bell, *Communitarianism and its Critics* (Oxford: Clarendon Press, 1993).

Tony Benn, 'The Moral Basis of the Radical Left' in David Ormrod (ed.), *Fellowship, Freedom and Equality. Lectures in Memory of R. H. Tawney* (London: Christian Socialist Movement, 1990), pp. 103–9.

Anthony Black, *Guild and State: European Political Thought from the Twelfth Century to the Present* (New Brunswick: Transaction, 2003).

Jeremy Black, *Britain Since the Seventies: Politics and Society in the Consumer Age* (London: Reaktion Books, 2004).

Tony Blair, 'Forging a New Agenda' in *Marxism Today* (October 1991).

Tony Blair, *Constitutional Change and the Future of Britain* (London: Charter 88 Trust, 1992).

Tony Blair, 'Why I am a Christian', *Sunday Telegraph* (7 April 1996).

Tony Blair, *New Britain. My Vision of a Young Country* (London: Fourth Estate, 1996).

Leonardo Boff, *Trinity and Society* (Tunbridge Wells: Burns and Oates, 1988).

Callum Brown, *The Death Of Christian Britain* (London: Routledge, 2001).

Chris Bryant, *Possible Dreams* (London: Hodder and Stoughton, 1996).

James Byrne (ed.), *The Christian Understanding of God Today* (Dublin: Columba, 1993).

Mark D. Chapman, 'Theology, Nationalism and the First World War: Christian Ethics and the Constraints of Politics' in *Studies in Christian Ethics* 8 (1995), pp. 13–35.

Mark D. Chapman, 'Concepts of the Voluntary Church in England and Germany, 1890–1920: A Study of J. N. Figgis and Ernst Troeltsch' in *Zeitschrift für neuere Theologiegeschichte* 2 (1995), pp. 37–59.

Mark D. Chapman, *Liturgy, Socialism and Life: The Legacy of Conrad Noel* (London: DLT, 2001).

Mark D. Chapman, *The Coming Crisis: The Impact of Eschatology on Edwardian England* (Sheffield: Sheffield Academic Press, 2001).

Chris Coates, *Utopia Britannica: British Utopian Experiments: 1325–1945* (London: Diggers and Dreamers, 2001).

David Coates and Joel Krieger, *Blair's War* (Cambridge: Polity, 2004).

C. A. R. Crosland, *The Future of Socialism* (London: Cape, 1956).

Grace Davie, *Religion in Modern Europe* (Oxford: Oxford University Press, 2000).

Alan Deacon, 'Self Interest and Collective Welfare: Frank Field and the Debate about the Future of Work' in Andrew R. Morton (ed.), *The Future of Welfare* (Edinburgh: Centre for Theology and Public Issues, 1997), pp. 119–32.

Stephen Driver and Luke Martell, *Blair's Britain* (Cambridge: Polity, 2002).

Amitai Etzioni, *The Spirit of Community: Rights, Responsibility and the Communitarian Agenda* (New York: Crown, 1993).

Paul S. Fiddes, *Participating in God. A Pastoral Doctrine of the Trinity* (London: DLT, 2000).

Frank Field, *Freedom and Wealth in a Socialist Future* (London: Constable, 1987).

Frank Field, *The Politics of Paradise. A Christian Approach to the Kingdom* (London: Fount, 1987).

Frank Field, 'Socialism and the Politics of Radial Distribution' in David Ormrod (ed.), *Fellowship, Freedom and Equality. Lectures in Memory of R. H. Tawney* (London: Christian Socialist Movement, 1990), pp. 49–58.

Frank Field, *An Agenda for Britain* (London: HarperCollins, 1993).

Frank Field, *Making Welfare Work. Reconstructing Welfare for the Millennium* (London: Institute of Community Studies, 1995).

Frank Field, 'Rejoinder' in Alan Deacon (ed.), *Stakeholder Welfare* (London: IEA, 1996).

Frank Field, 'Response to Alan Deacon' in Andrew R. Morton (ed.), *The Future of Welfare* (Edinburgh: Centre for Theology and Public Issues, 1997), pp. 141–53.

Frank Field, 'What Then Was Unthinkable?' in *Crucible* 38 (1999), pp. 16–30.

J. N. Figgis, 'Erastus and Erastianism' in *Journal of Theological Studies* 2 (1901), pp. 66–101.

J. N. Figgis, 'Political Thought in the Sixteenth Century' in *Cambridge Modern History*, III, ed. Lord Acton (Cambridge: Cambridge University Press, 1904), pp. 736–69.

J. N. Figgis, *From Gerson to Grotius* (Cambridge: Cambridge University Press, 1907).

J. N. Figgis, *The Gospel and Human Needs* (London: Longmans, 1909).

J. N. Figgis, *Civilisation at the Cross Roads*, Four Lectures delivered before Harvard University in the year 1911 on the William Belden Noble Foundation (London: Longmans, 1912).

J. N. Figgis, *Antichrist and Other Sermons* (London: Longmans, 1913).

J. N. Figgis, *Churches in the Modern State* (London: Longmans, 1914).

J. N. Figgis, *The Fellowship of the Mystery* (London: Longmans, 1914).

J. N. Figgis, *Hopes for English Religion* (London: Longmans, 1919).

Duncan Forrester, 'Welfare and Conviction Politics' in Andrew R. Morton (ed.), *The Future of Welfare* (Edinburgh: Centre for Theology and Public Issues, 1997), pp. 133–40.

Ernest Gellner, 'The Importance of Being Modular' in J. A. Hall (ed.), *Civil Society: Theory, History, Comparison* (Cambridge: Polity, 1995), pp. 32–55.

Anthony Giddens, *The Third Way. The Renewal of Social Democracy* (Cambridge: Polity, 1998). German translation: *Der dritte Weg. Die Erneuerung der sozialen Demokratie* (Frankfurt-am-Main: Suhrkamp, 1999).

Otto von Gierke, *Political Theories of the Middle Ages* (Cambridge: Cambridge University Press, 1900).

Robin Gill, *Moral Communities* (Exeter: Exeter University Press, 1992).

S. T. Glass, *The Responsible Society* (London: Longmans, 1966).

John Gray, *False Dawn. The Delusions of Global Capitalism* (London: Granta, 1999).

John Gray, *Two Faces of Liberalism* (New York: New Press, 2000).

Matthew Grimley, *Citizenship, Community, and the Church of England* (Oxford: Clarendon, 2004).

Reg Groves, *Conrad Noel and the Thaxted Movement. An Adventure in Christian Socialism* (New York: Augustus M. Keeley, 1968).

Colin Gunton, *The One, The Three and the Many. God, Creation and the Culture of Modernity* (Cambridge: Cambridge University Press, 1993).

Colin Gunton, *The Promise of Trinitarian Theology* (Edinburgh: T & T Clark, 1993).

Jürgen Habermas, *The Theory of Communicative Action* (Cambridge: Polity, 1987).

Jürgen Habermas, *Autonomy and Solidarity* (London: Verso, 1992).

Paul Hirst, *Associative Democracy* (Cambridge: Polity, 1994).

Paul Hirst, *From Statism to Pluralism* (London: UCL Press, 1997).

Eric Hobsbawm, *Nations and Nationalism: Programme, Myth, Reality* (Cambridge: Cambridge University Press, 1992).

David Hollenbach sj, *The Common Good and Christian Ethics* (Cambridge: Cambridge University Press, 2003).

K. C. Hsaio, *Political Pluralism* (London: Kegan Paul, 1927).

H. J. Laski, *Studies in the Problem of Sovereignty* (New Haven: Yale University Press, 1917).

H. J. Laski, *Authority in the Modern State* (New Haven: Yale University Press, 1919).

H. J. Laski, *The Foundations of Sovereignty and Other Essays* (London: Allen and Unwin, 1921).

Kenneth Leech, *The Social God* (London: Sheldon Press, 1981).

Kenneth Leech, *The Sky is Red* (London: DLT, 1997).

George Lindbeck, *The Nature of Doctrine: Religion and Theology in a Postliberal Age* (London: SPCK, 1984).

Gerhard Lohfink, *Jesus and Community: The Social Dimension of Christian Faith* (Philadelphia: Fortress, 1984).

Alasdair MacIntyre, *After Virtue* (London: Duckworth, 1981).

Alastair MacIntyre, 'A Partial Response to My Critics' in John Horton and Susan Mendus (eds), *After MacIntyre* (Cambridge: Polity, 1994), pp. 283–304.

James Mackey, 'Are There Christian Alternatives to Trinitarian Thinking?' in James Byrne (ed.), *The Christian Understanding of God Today* (Dublin: Columba, 1993), pp. 66–75.

Iain McLean, *Rational Choice and British Politics. An Analysis of Rhetoric and Manipulation from Peel to Blair* (Oxford: Oxford University Press, 2001).

John Macmurray, *Conditions of Freedom* (London: Faber, 1956).

John Macmurray, *Persons in Relation* (London: Faber, 1961).

H. M. Magid, *English Political Pluralism* (New York: Columbia University Press, 1941).

David Marquand, *Taming Leviathan: Social Democracy and Decentralisation* (London: Socialist Commentary Publications, 1980).

David Marquand, *The New Reckoning. Capitalism, States and Citizens* (Cambridge: Polity, 1997).

David Marquand, *Decline of the Public* (Cambridge: Polity, 2004).

Jürgen Moltmann, *The Crucified God* (London: SCM, 1974).

Jürgen Moltmann, *The Trinity and the Kingdom of God* (London: SCM, 1981).

Jürgen Moltmann, 'The Social Doctrine of the Trinity' in James Byrne (ed.), *The Christian Understanding of God Today* (Dublin: Columba, 1993), pp. 110–111.

Andrew R. Morton (ed.), *The Future of Welfare* (Edinburgh: Centre for Theology and Public Issues, 1997).

Michael Newman, *Harold Laski. A Political Biography* (Basingstoke: Macmillan, 1993).

David Nicholls, *The Pluralist State* (London: Macmillan, 1975).

David Nicholls, *Deity and Domination* (London: Routledge, 1989).

David Nicholls, 'Trinity and Conflict' in *Theology* XCVI (1993), pp. 19–27.

Conrad Noel, *The Battle of the Flags. A Study in Christian Politics* (London: The Labour Publishing House, 1922).

Conrad Noel, *Jesus The Heretic* (London: J. M. Dent, 1939).

Conrad Noel, *An Autobiography*, edited by Sydney Dark (London: J. M. Dent, 1945).

Metropolitan Geevarghese Mar Osthathios, *Theology of a Classless Society* (Guildford: Lutterworth Press, 1979).

Thomas D. Parker, 'The Political Meaning of the Doctrine of the Trinity: some theses' in *Journal of Religion* 60 (1980), pp. 165–84.

G. P. H. Pawson CR, *Edward Keble Talbot. His Community and His Friends* (London: SPCK, 1954).

Derek Philips, *Looking Backward: A Critical Appraisal of Communitarian Thought* (Princeton: Princeton University Press, 1993).

Ronald Preston, *Religion and the Persistence of Capitalism* (London: SCM, 1979).

John Rentoul, *Tony Blair* (London: Warner Books, 1996).

W. H. Riker, *The Art of Political Manipulation* (New Haven: Yale University Press, 1986).

Richard H. Roberts, *Religion, Theology and the Human Sciences* (Cambridge: Cambridge University Press, 2001).

Jonathan Sacks, *The Persistence of Faith* (London: Weidenfeld and Nicolson, 1992).

Adam B. Seligman, *The Problem of Trust* (Princeton: Princeton University Press, 1997).

John Sopel, *Tony Blair. The Moderniser* (London: Bantam, 1995).

Mervyn Stockwood, *The Cross and the Sickle* (London: Sheldon Press, 1978).

Roland N. Stromberg, *Redemption by War. The Intellectuals and 1914* (Lawrence: Regent's Press of Kansas, 1982).

N. P. Sykes, *The English Religious Tradition* (London: SCM, 1953).

William Temple, *The Education of Citizens* (London: Parents' National Educational Union, 1905).

William Temple, *Christianity and the State* (London: Macmillan, 1928).

William Temple, *Citizen and Churchman* (London: Eyre and Spottiswoode, 1941).

William Temple, *Christianity and Social Order* (Harmondsworth: Penguin, 1942).

Ferdinand Tönnies, *Community and Civil Society*, translated by José Harris and M. Hollis (Cambridge: Cambridge University Press, 2001).

Fran Tonkiss and Andrew Passey (eds), *Trust and Civil Society* (Basingstoke, Macmillan, 2000).

Maurice G. Tucker, *John Neville Figgis. A Study* (London: SPCK, 1950).

Andrew Vincent and Raymond Plant, *Philosophy, Politics and Citizenship* (Oxford: Blackwell, 1984).

Wendy Wheeler, 'Dangerous Business' in Mark Perryman (ed.), *The Blair Agenda* (London: Lawrence and Wishart, 1996), pp. 100–124.

Gordon White, 'Civil Society, Democratization and Development' in *Democratization* I (1994), pp. 375–90.

Andrew Whiteford and Michael McGrath, *The Distribution of Income in South Africa* (Pretoria: Human Sciences Research Council, 1994).

Alan Wilkinson, *The Community of the Resurrection. A Centenary History* (London: SCM, 1992).

David Willetts, *Blair's Gurus* (London: Centre for Policy Studies, 1996).

Rowan Williams, 'The Literal Sense of Scripture' in *Modern Theology* 7 (1991), pp. 121–34.

Robert Woodifield, 'Conrad Noel' in Maurice B. Reckitt (ed.), *For Christ and People* (London: SPCK, 1968).

Barbara Wootton, *In a World I Never Made* (London: Allen and Unwin, 1967).

E. and S. Yeo, 'On the Uses of Community from Owenism to the Present' in Stephen Yeo (ed.), *New Views of Co-operation* (London: Routledge, 1988), pp. 229–58.

John Zizioulas, *Being as Communion. Studies in Personhood and the Church* (London: DLT, 1985).

INDEX

Alternative Service Book 63
anomie 61
associationalism 92–5

Benn, Tony 82
Beveridge Report 78
Blair, Tony *passim*
  and Christianity 15–21
  and community 13–29, 99
  and democracy 62–4
  and management 30–2, 36–7
  and New Labour 5–7
  and war 62
Boff, Leonardo 45–6
Booth, Cherie 17
Brown, Callum 22
Brown, Gordon 30, 35–6
Buiter, William 36
Bush, George W. 29

Campbell, Alastair 33
Clause Four 6–7
civil society 67, 71–6
Clinton, Bill 25
Cold War 61
Cole, G. D. H. 76, 84
common good 16, 62–4, 66, 69–70,
  98, 100
Common Worship 63
communitarianism 71–3, 94, 106n
community 12–29, 59–100
community centres 12
Community of the Resurrection 84,
  92
conflict 29, 50–8, 60

Creighton, Mandell 84
Cromwell, Thomas 41
Crosland, Anthony 7, 29, 77

Dahrendorf, Ralf 97
dechristianisation 21
divine right of kings 42, 84, 87, 90–1
Durkheim, Émile 22, 60

Etzioni, Amitai 72
exclusion 59

Faith in the City 13
Fiddes, Paul 53–4
Field, Frank 76–82, 94, 95, 98, 107n,
  108n
  Politics of Paradise 80–2
Figgis, John Neville 84–92, 98
  and authority of the church 86–90
  biography 84–5, 92, 109n
  Churches in the Modern State 86–8,
    110n, 111n
  and conciliarism 86, 111n
  and fraternity 92
  and freedom 91–2
first world war 61, 106n

Gellner, Ernst 96
Giddens, Anthony 26
Gill, Robin 72
Global Ethics Foundation 17–21, 36
guilds 94, 111n
Gunton, Colin 48–9

Habermas, Jürgen 72

Hardie, Keir 27
Hattersley, Roy 7
Henry VIII 42, 76
'heresthetic rhetoric' 34, 98
Hirst, Paul 84, 94, 95

Ingham, Bernard 33
Iraq 29

Kinnock, Neil 7
Küng, Hans 17, 36

Laski, Harold, 40, 84, 97
Leech, Kenneth 45
Lindbeck, George 52
Lohfink, Gerhard 71

MacIntyre, Alasdair 41, 72
Mackey, James 54
McLean, Iain 34
Macmurray, John 16, 49, 105n
Maitland, F. W. 84
management 30–42, 93, 97
Marquand, David 23–4
Masterman, Charles 60
May Day 1–4
Mbeki, Thabo 65–6, 68
Millennium Dome 40–1
Moltmann, Jürgen 46–8, 53–5
Monetary Policy Committee 35–6, 38
'Moral Regeneration Movement'
    64–9
Morris, William 24
Murray, Shirley 63

nationalism 61–2, 106n
National Trust 73, 96
Newbigin, Lesslie 80
New Labour 3–7, 9, 31, 74, 99
Ngubane, Ben 68
Nicholls, David 54–6, 84
Noel, Conrad 43–5, 104n

Osthathios, Geevarghese Mar 48

Parker, Thomas D. 49–50
Philip and James, SS. 1

Plant, Raymond 22
political pluralism 76, 83–100, 109n
Portillo, Michael 1
Preston, Ronald 11
Progressive Governance 24–6

Quality Assurance Agency 39
quangos 31–42

Riker, W. H. 34

Sacks, Jonathan 71, 72
Saint-Simon, Henri de 23
Schröder, Gerhard 25
September 11, 26–7, 62
social doctrine of the Trinity 43–58
South Africa 64–9
sovereignty 75–6
stakeholders 78, 94, 95, 96, 97
Stockwood, Mervyn 2
Straw, Jack 26
subsidiarity 96
Sykes, Norman 87–8

Tawney, R. H. 8, 78
Temple, William 8–11, 14, 16, 31, 81
    Christianity and Social Order 8–10
Thatcher, Margaret 31–4, 94
'There is no alternative' 32–5, 37
Third Way 24–6
Thomson, Peter 16
toleration 88
Tutu, Desmond 69
Twigg, Stephen 1

Weber, Max 60
welfare state 7–11, 28, 77
Whitley Report 96
Willets, David 77
Williams, Rowan 52
Wootton, Barbara 79

Zizioulas, John 49
Zuma, Jacob 66–7